Stepping Out

IMPROVING LITERACY –

D1646955

A Whole School Approach to Literacy

in secondary schools

developed by
Pat Kiddey
Greg Robson

for
Education Department
of Western Australia

Supporting your Professional Development

GHPD

©2001 Education Department of Western Australia

ISBN 0 435 04708 6

Cataloguing-in-publication data
A catalogue record for this book is available from the British Library.

GHPD

Published by GHPD
Ginn Heinemann Professional Development
Halley Court, Jordan Hill, Oxford OX2 8EJ
www.ghpd.co.uk

2001   2000   2002

5   4   3   2   1

Design and artwork production: Serif Tree · Oxford
Illustrations: Celia Hart
Printed and bound in Great Britain by:
Ashford Colour Press, Gosport Hants

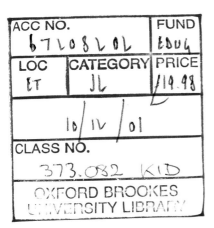

Preface

Stepping Out is a literacy professional development program designed specifically for teachers in middle and secondary schools. While school systems around the world define the phases of schooling in different ways, the pupils for whom *Stepping Out* is designed are those between 10–16 years of age – the adolescent years. *Stepping Out* assists teachers, subject departments and whole school staff to implement and monitor literacy improvement plans. It has been implemented extensively in middle and secondary schools in Western Australia, and acknowledges the long-term nature of literacy improvement. All components of the program link closely to classroom practice and clearly show how literacy strategies can be incorporated within subject specific content.

In 1998, the Education Department of Western Australia contracted Edith Cowan University to manage several of its major educational programs. The University established ECU Resources for Learning, Ltd. as its operating company for this purpose. The Education Department retains the intellectual property of its resources.

During 1998, ECU RL undertook a major review of *Stepping Out* session notes, materials and resources. Materials needing revision were modified; new curriculum initiatives and materials were incorporated and further texts were written to support the professional development program. Further modules and texts will be added in subsequent years. The review was a collaborative process involving teachers from the Education Department of Western Australia and participating schools and academics from Edith Cowan University. The final result is a practical, professional development program of international quality.

This edition of *Stepping Out* was prepared with the specific needs of U.K. schools in mind. There is a focus on the Key Stage 3 component of the National Literacy Strategy.

Greg Robson
Chief Executive Officer
Edith Cowan University Resources for Learning
Western Australia

Acknowledgements

The *Stepping Out* resource was developed by the Education Department of Western Australia.

This text, *A Whole School Approach to Literacy*, was developed by:

Pat Kiddey
Greg Robson
(Edith Cowan University Resources for Learning)

The input of the following people is acknowledged and valued:

Associate Professor Judith Rivalland, Associate Professor William Louden, Dr Mary Rohl, Dr Marion Milton and Ken Willis
(Academic staff from Edith Cowan University, Western Australia)

The General Strategies section of this text was developed by Pat Kiddey and Felicity Waring, (ECU Resources for Learning). It incorporates a selection of strategies from the original *Stepping Out* Literacy and Learning Strategies book, developed by Adele Bradley, for the Education Department of Western Australia (1995).

Contents

What is the purpose of this text?

Improving Learning in the Middle and Secondary School is a component of *Stepping Out*, a resource designed to support school systems, schools and teachers as they strive to improve pupils' literacy and learning outcomes. The purpose of the text is to highlight key issues related to the specific context of middle and secondary schools, and to raise the awareness of teachers, school leaders, professional development consultants and researchers about factors that impact on teaching, learning and assessment in these contexts.

Improving literacy standards during the middle and secondary schooling years is not something that happens in isolation. An important premise of *Stepping Out* is that a critical component of the improvement process is to understand clearly the context in which learning occurs at this phase of schooling. A clear depiction of the context is provided in this text, along with practical suggestions for how, and where, the improvement effort might be focused.

The text comprises two sections:

> *Improving Learning in the Middle and Secondary School*, which provides the context for all *Stepping Out* professional development modules.

> *Literacy and Learning Strategies*, which highlights a range of process strategies that can be used to support teachers as they tackle the literacy demands of subject areas.

This text was also designed to assist UK schools in addressing Key Stage 3 requirements of the National Literacy Strategy. It is part of a series of *Stepping Out* professional development modules and is used as a resource document (and required reading) for participants.

Improving Learning in the Middle and Secondary School

1 Introduction

The National Literacy Strategy seeks to raise standards of achievement in all subject areas, by raising pupils' literacy skills. The Key Stage 3 component focuses on curriculum continuity from Year 6 (P7) to Year 7 (S1), targeted support for pupils experiencing difficulties and the explicit teaching of literacy skills. Middle and secondary schools are required to build on work carried out in primary schools, to share understandings and information about teaching, learning and assessment, and to provide intervention programmes and input at summer schools for pupils who are underachieving.

A range of powerful factors often combine to make the years of middle and secondary schooling a difficult period for learning. Each one of these factors can have a direct impact on pupils' learning outcomes. Most educators will agree with the claim that early adolescence is a period when achievement seems to stand still, or even decline, for many pupils. It is an obvious yet poignant reality. What is not so certain, and where there is continuing debate, is how the different factors interact, which factors are the most influential, and what the best ways are of addressing the challenges that confront teachers during this most vexing phase of schooling.

There are three questions, then, for educators interested in the middle and secondary years:

- What makes it so difficult to learn in these contexts?
- How well do we understand middle and secondary school contexts?
- What might be done to improve learning during this phase?

What makes learning difficult in the middle and secondary school context?

So what is it that makes it difficult to learn in these contexts? Why do a significant number of adolescent learners make little progress academically after their first year at secondary school? Is it because of their unique physical, emotional and psychological needs, or their unpredictable hormones? Is it the culture shock of moving to a different organisational structure that promotes a heavily subject-orientated curriculum? Or is it that the literacy demands they have to tackle in each learning area become more complex?

It is tempting for teachers to answer each of these questions in the affirmative, but if that is the case, the significance of the challenge increases – to a point where the problems seem overwhelming.

How well do we understand the context of middle and secondary schooling?

What kinds of understandings do consultants, researchers and teachers have about the ways in which these different factors impact on learning in the middle and secondary school context? Much has been written about adolescent learners and about the way their schooling is organised. However, it has proved difficult to maintain a concentrated focus on the particular context of this phase of schooling. Whether this is because it is a genuinely difficult phase to come to grips with, or whether the early years are regarded as more fertile ground for providing resources and initiating reform efforts is difficult to judge.

What does stand out is the lack of concentrated effort and attention given to this phase of schooling over significant periods of time. Even when there are clear understandings about the different factors that affect learning in the middle and secondary years, it seems as if the issues related to this context continue to be taken for granted.

It is difficult to understand any of the issues without being fully aware of the context in which they exist. Similarly, it is difficult to understand the issues without a critical understanding of the diverse needs of adolescent learners and the growing demands placed on pupils' literacy skills at this phase of their schooling.

What can be done to improve the situation?

What might reduce the difficulties that so many adolescent learners experience in the secondary school? Perhaps improved teaching and a move away from such a heavy emphasis on acquiring curriculum content would assist. Do school leaders need to look at different ways of organising school structures, classes and timetables? There might also be benefits in improving links between learning areas (subjects), in engaging in more effective professional development programmes and in providing opportunities for teachers to work collaboratively with one another.

These are not new issues. Whatever the strategy or blend of ideas that schools adopt, it seems unlikely that a small or a simple effort will have much of an impact. The issues are large, and too many teachers feel that they are beyond their capacity to tackle. What does seem clear is that, whatever the scale of the solution, there is a need for practical tools and support structures that can operate on many levels.

We can expect little change unless teachers and school administrators do become more aware of the ways in which the context of the middle and secondary school impacts on learning.

2 The middle and secondary school context

The middle and secondary years of schooling (often dubbed the forgotten, Cinderella stage of schooling) are currently under scrutiny in a number of countries around the world. Increasing pressure is being placed on governments, schools and teachers to improve standards. The pressure in the UK is fuelled by the requirements of Key Stage 3 of the National Literacy Strategy, the publication of league tables and the fact that school funding is now linked to improvement. Many schools have implemented innovative and successful programmes for pupils at this stage of schooling, but a significant number continue to fall through the net. Closer scrutiny has revealed an 'over-riding impression of insufficient attention, if not neglect, towards the schooling needs of adolescents' (Berkley, 1994).

To understand why it is difficult to achieve reform at this stage of schooling and why it is much harder for pupils to learn in the middle and secondary school, it is necessary to view the context from a variety of perspectives. This section outlines the factors that form the unique context of the middle and secondary school. It is organised around the following perspectives:

– What the journey from primary to middle and secondary school looks like
– Ability and achievement ranges
– Achievement and attitude changes
– Key aspects of middle and secondary school organisation
– The context outside the school.

Each perspective has significant implications for educational leaders, schools and teachers.

What the journey from primary to middle and secondary school looks like

Primary school pupils generally like school. They are accepted socially by their peers, get on well with their teachers, enjoy doing schoolwork, and view the curriculum as something that is useful and relevant (Hill, 1993, p.14). They enjoy being at the top of the 'pecking order' in their last year of school, and relish the extra responsibilities and privileges that their seniority brings. They also reap the benefits of learning in a smaller, nurturing environment with one teacher, and one group of pupils. Their teacher is specifically trained in pedagogy, and is usually familiar with a wide range of strategies that enhance learning.

Flexible time allocations in the primary school make it possible for teachers to incorporate innovative methods of teaching and to plan a multidisciplinary or integrated curriculum. Their pupils' pastoral care and learning needs are easier to identify, because pupils are routinely observed working in a range of different contexts, over longer periods of time. There are plenty of opportunities for pupils to talk and work collaboratively with others, because the majority of primary classrooms are set up to facilitate small group learning.

Moving into the middle and secondary context

When the same pupils arrive at the middle or secondary school, they immediately become the youngest, most inexperienced and most powerless of the school population. The culture shock they experience during this transition process can be similar to the culture shock experienced when moving from Hawaii to Bosnia (Hargreaves, 1998). They have to adjust to a larger sized campus, to new surroundings, to a more impersonal culture, to a diverse curriculum, to new ways of learning, and to a different organisational structure. The differences between primary and secondary school contexts are stark, even though pupils from both sectors are chronologically similar.

There is a sharp contrast between pupils' primary and secondary school experiences. The curriculum shifts from being generalised and integrated, to being structured and specific. It becomes 'more concepts' based. Tight timelines mean that learners are often required to take on a more passive role, and that the pedagogy gets narrower.

The first year of secondary school is probably the most difficult, because of:

– the increased amount of reading in all subject areas

– an increased difficulty in level of concepts in all readings
– variations in teaching methods which each new subject teacher presents
– comparatively large classes which make individual assistance difficult either before or after lessons
– peer pressure, which prohibits being identified as needing assistance, let alone accepting any prolonged help.

Of course, many primary pupils make the transfer across the 'divide' with a minimum of fuss. They make friends easily and enjoy having a variety of teachers and a range of subjects to choose from. However, a significant number have more trouble adapting to the secondary school context, because the move from class to class every 50 minutes makes it difficult to establish new and effective relationships with their teachers and their peers.

Over the period of one day, pupils can have four to six different teachers, each of whom is likely to have a different teaching style and a different set of expectations. It is also extremely difficult for teachers to build up detailed knowledge about individual pupils' learning needs when they are required to interact with up to six different groups a day.

Ability and achievement ranges

In primary school, different levels of achievement between pupils can be expected. By middle school, these differences can also be expected, but are often magnified. Those pupils who have mastered the basic tools of learning can apply them to learn new concepts as the curriculum becomes more demanding. Those who are still struggling to come to grips with the basic skills face the prospect of falling further behind their peers. Gaps in ability widen. Barber (1999) suggests that a 'significant number of "lost boys" who fail to learn to read and write well by age 11 never recover educationally'.

What may seem like small differences in achievement in the early years can be accentuated when pupils reach the secondary school. The developmental diversity of this age group makes it difficult to organise an educational programme that adequately meets the needs of all. It is often more difficult in the middle and secondary school to observe whether pupils are making progress, because achievement tends to be more subtle in the adolescent years, compared to the breakthroughs and developmental leaps associated with early learners.

In addition, an increasing array of descriptions – for pupils with specific learning difficulties, those with ADD, or those from differing cultural backgrounds – adds to the perceptions of teachers that, at this point, pupil diversity seems to have expanded in many different directions at once, and so the puzzle of static or low achievement remains.

Achievement and attitude changes

The majority of primary pupils start their middle and secondary schooling with great enthusiasm, but by the end of their first year, many begin to show a 'dip' in their achievement and attitude to learning. The problem tends to compound the following year, as the same pupils become bored and uninspired by their school work, and wholly preoccupied with friendships. As a result, their marks drop, they develop a poor image of themselves as learners and fall even further behind. An anti-work peer group culture can develop, without an appreciation that working hard now will make a real difference to achievement later. Unfortunately, these negative minority groups can have a considerable impact on the culture of the larger cohort of pupils (Rudduck *et al.*, 1996).

There is a significant body of research on adolescents' attitudes to school. One detailed study of 460 pupils (Kirkpatrick, 1995) found that their academic performance tended to taper off once they reached secondary school, that their learning outcomes in English and mathematics did not improve during their first year in the new context, and that there was a negative change in their attitude towards academic work. The study revealed the following perceptions that pupils had about secondary school:

- It was more important to submit work on time than to concentrate on 'doing their best'.
- They were expected to *complete,* rather than *learn,* a large volume of work.
- Content was covered rapidly, encouraging superficial approaches to learning and work avoidance behaviour.
- Standards and expectations weren't 'spelt out'. Opportunities to use other pupils' work as guidelines or models weren't used.
- There were fewer opportunities to participate in group work than at primary school. They felt that this denied them opportunities for learning informally about standards of performance, and about different learning strategies.
- Feedback from teachers tended to be limited – rather than informative or instructive.
- Links were not always made with what had previously been learned in primary school. Pupils considered they had 'done' the work before, and therefore there was no need to exert any effort.
- There were fewer opportunities for them to engage in independent work, and self-regulate their learning behaviours.
- The organisation of the secondary classroom and timetable made it difficult for them to discuss academic work with their teachers in a discreet manner.

Barber (1999) suggests that when pupils arrive in the secondary school they are often tested so that a new baseline for learning can be established. Because the pupils have had a break and find themselves in a new, uncertain environment, they tend to score less well. Secondary teachers may then assume that the primary school records were wrong, and aim their teaching at the new, low baseline established by tests. Thus low expectations can be built in from the start.

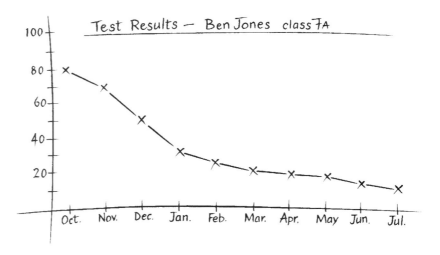

In summary then, pupils are generally much less positive about school by the end of their first year of secondary school. Some exhibit a decline in attitude and performance, and this less than positive attitude can soon turn to disenchantment and alienation.

Whilst many pupils thrive in the middle and secondary school context, others do not find it to be a rewarding experience. They engage in negative 'trying out' behaviour, neglect to hand in assignments and start to skip classes. Their marks decline rapidly and the gaps in their learning widen. Some pupils whose behaviour is not usually problematic can also find schoolwork 'boring' and start falling behind. These pupils also become disengaged from their learning and gain little from their schooling experience.

Disengagement can occur for a variety of reasons. It is often difficult to detect, define and measure, and it can change over time. Unfortunately, relationships with other pupils and with teachers can be affected in the meantime, and some of the things they need to learn, and want to learn, are bypassed. There is a danger that pupils who are 'different' from other pupils can be labelled as alienated.

> *Adolescence, by its very nature, engenders conflict and inconsistencies that can result in feelings of alienation, powerlessness and frustration.*

> (Earle and Hargreaves, 1990, p.206)

There is a clear need to minimise the degree of alienation that occurs in middle and secondary schools. This can be achieved, not by simply engaging in dialogue about problems, failures and shortcomings of the system, but by reducing curriculum, pedagogical and school organisational factors that impact on pupils' learning outcomes at this phase of schooling.

Key aspects of secondary school organisation

Timetabling

Time is organised differently in secondary schools. The large number of pupils and the need to match specialist teachers to groups of pupils cause secondary schools to place the 'timetable' at the forefront of their planning and organisation. Timetabling constraints can place severe limits on innovative teaching practice. By the time the class has settled, late-comers have been accommodated, the roll has been taken, and links have been made to the last lesson, a considerable amount of learning/teaching time has already been absorbed. Forty or fifty-minute periods make if difficult for teachers to retain continuity, rigour and consistency between lessons, because it can be days before they are with the same group of pupils again. Time constraints also make it difficult for them to develop effective working relationships with pupils, to implement integrated learning programmes, to team teach with their peers, and for pupils to spend the time that is required to work through processes that lead to better learning.

It is difficult for teachers in the middle and secondary school context to find time to work collaboratively with each other. Time is tight, and teachers are often unable to share teaching experiences, plan cross-curriculum learning programmes, share their skills, knowledge and expertise, or analyse issues related to individual and groups of pupils that they all teach.

The daily routine in some schools has often been likened to a production line:

> *Pupils come onto the production line at approximately 9am, and during the first few periods, have an English component instilled, followed by a maths, science, humanities, creative arts, technology component and so on. Up to five or six components might be fitted over the period of a day, with teachers having limited knowledge of the learning that preceded or followed their input.*

(Morgan, 1993)

Some pupils find that moving around to large numbers of teachers, and working within inflexible timetables and in rigid pupil groupings, reduce their capacity to learn effectively. It might help if the school day was simplified and/or if greater flexibility was introduced to groupings, because some pupils develop more rapidly than others. A more personalised approach to teaching might also be appreciated.

Structures

Traditional secondary school classes and timetables tend to be organised in much the same way as they were organised 20 or 30 years ago, despite the fact that they now cater for the needs of a very different generation of pupils.

> *If you walked into a (high) school today, you'd know just what to do. It looks very similar to the way it was. There are more subjects to be taken, but the organisation, the division of learning along neat subject faculty lines, the 40 minute lesson, the changeovers – the sheer impersonality of it all – is alive and well.*

(Eyers *et al.*, 1992)

In many secondary contexts, pupils are exposed to a curriculum divided into discrete units or subject area compartments, to a large number of subject areas and to a wide range of specialist teachers. Teachers from different subject areas teach in separate classrooms and can often be unaware of what is being taught elsewhere in the school.

Consequently, links that help pupils to establish wider views of topics, or enrich their understandings, skills and knowledge, are seldom made across the curriculum. Learning can become fragmented if schools are not careful, because pupils pick up small chunks of information from each learning area, and are not always given the opportunity to see the whole picture. Even if the learning experiences themselves are extremely effective, it is difficult for pupils to make meaningful connections across subject areas if few links are made between subjects or to their own life experiences. When they encounter disconnected and fragmented learning on a daily, weekly and yearly basis, they have to make many of the links themselves.

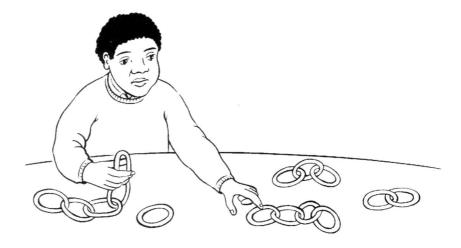

The effect of different organisational structures on school culture

The traditional structure of secondary schools, perhaps more than any other structure, seems to impact sharply on what teachers do and how pupils respond. The way a school is organised imposes limits on how teachers work together to exchange ideas, to share information about pupils and to become involved in decision making.

Of course, organisational structures do not automatically determine what happens in a school – people do – but they do influence the culture significantly. Fullan and Hargreaves (1991), in their analysis of secondary schooling, capture precisely the contrasting cultures that can emerge as a result of different organisational structures. At one end of the continuum, the culture can be characterised as 'fragmented individualism', as represented in the following diagram:

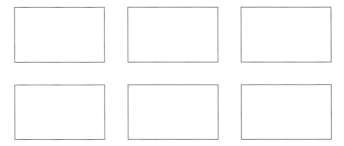

Fragmented individualism

Teachers in this type of culture tend to work alone in their classrooms, in professional isolation. They construct learning programmes and evaluate their success as separate, stand alone 'units of delivery'. The only meaningful feedback they receive about the effectiveness of their teaching comes from their own observations of the pupils they teach.

This means that there is a ceiling limit on the effectiveness and innovation of their teaching practice which is confined to their own experiences, their own interpretations, and their own motivation to seek improvement. Inevitably, this type of organisational structure results in a narrower range of teaching practices.

Further along the continuum, Fullan and Hargreaves describe what they term as a 'balkanised culture', represented in the diagram below. In this environment, departments or faculties tend to operate as separate, sometimes competing groups within the school. This reduces teachers' collective capacities, restricts opportunities for them to share their knowledge and experiences, and reduces openness, trust and support between teachers from different subject departments. In this type of organisation, there is potential for teachers to have inconsistent expectations for pupils' performance across the school, and for there to be poor continuity in monitoring pupils' progress.

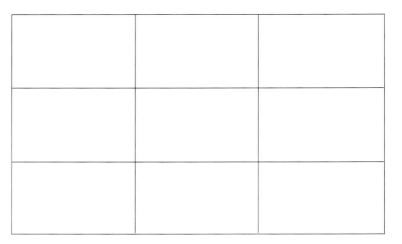

Balkanised groups

By contrast, at a further point along the cultural continuum, Fullan and Hargreaves describe a 'collaborative' secondary school culture. Teachers in this environment recognise that teaching is difficult, and that giving and receiving help does not imply incompetence. They flesh out issues together in order to reach agreement, and seek continuous improvement in their teaching. They examine their existing practices critically, continuously trial and modify their programmes, seek better alternatives, and work hard to bring about improvement in their teaching, and in pupils' learning. This type of collaborative culture tends to be more receptive to change.

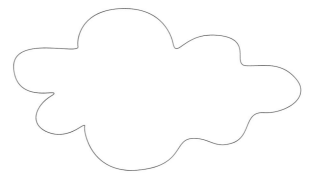

Collaborative culture

Imagine that you can become a better teacher, just by virtue of being on the staff of a particular school; – just for that one fact alone.

(Little, 1990, cited in Fullan and Hargreaves, 1991, p.46)

Differences between schools

The way we organise our schools impacts on the school culture, on the quality of teaching and ultimately, on pupils' learning outcomes. The degree to which the school culture is affected by the organisational structure of the school will differ from context to context, and the challenge for schools is to analyse critically the impact of their own organisational structures on pupils' learning.

It may be easy for some schools to change the way they work. However, for many teachers and for many schools, the issues require a great deal of patience and effort and are not easy to address. Improving the way in which schools work is something valuable to target, but it tends to happen over time. Whilst the efforts of individuals, departments and key stakeholders are essential to achieving such reform, it is not likely to happen immediately. In the meantime, teachers have to work within their existing school culture and organisation to effect improvement in learning. Many schools have tried different ways of organising the learning environment to cater for the needs of adolescent learners. They have clustered pupils in various primary/secondary configurations, set up sub-schools and teaching teams, made the timetable more flexible, and integrated the curriculum.

There is, however, no simple recipe or solution. Implementing change requires flexible approaches and a will to try alternative courses of action. The precise combination of elements that work in any one particular school would depend on the needs of that school.

What is needed is a clear understanding of the unique nature of adolescent pupils, and of the various factors that combine to form the complex context of the middle and secondary school. Schools might promote a healthy culture of examining current practice and identifying how their organisational structures and timetabling processes impact on pupils' learning. They could collect data to inform the planning and implementing of strategies that minimise barriers to learning. The same type of analysis would identify options and possibilities for engaging pupils in their own learning and for giving them responsibility for making decisions about their learning programme.

The context outside the school

Schooling does not happen in a vacuum. At this stage of their development, adolescents are trying to establish new relationships when their life is characterised by storm, crisis and harmony. They are likely to run into different sets of relationship issues as they test boundaries and question authority. If there is to be any conflict that strains family relationships, this is the time when it is most likely to occur. The conflict is not necessarily restricted to parents – it is likely to occur with other authority figures, such as teachers, police or sports coaches.

For many pupils, life outside school is infinitely more exciting than life at school. Their attachment to peers is extremely powerful, and many are part of the subculture of groups and gangs. Each of these different groups can have different ways of dressing, using language and behaviour. At this age they are also deeply entrenched in pop and media culture, in digital learning technologies, in music, fashion, teenage magazines and television soaps. This world is often left outside when they enter school, and therefore learning tends to be something that is disconnected from their personal experience.

> *When was the last time you heard someone claim that school education is routinely exciting, engaging and stimulating for students, that it provides the kind of rush that comes from theatre or music or competitive sport, that it regularly takes students so close to the edge of their experience that they get stage fright? When did school last seem slightly dangerous, a place that would give you a nervous thrill like the thrill you get from taking risks and going beyond your limits. In the iconography of contemporary life, school is the grey cardigan, sensible shoes, making sure you have a hanky, going to bed early, wearing clean underwear in case you get hit by a bus, and chewing each mouthful 32 times. It is the part of Western tradition that assumes that what you enjoy cannot be good for you, and what is good for you cannot be fun … Schooling is … the grey cardigan and the sensible shoes compared with the sparkle and sequins of popular culture.*

(Wilson, 1999, p.3)

This particular generation of pupils is being prepared for a future of change and uncertainty. The breadth of the social context within which they are located and the challenges and pressures they face today are far greater than earlier generations of pupils. There are changes in family structures, in the types of employment that they can access, and in the nature of learning technologies. Schools are trying to do more, with limited resources. Even the nature of learning has become more complex. The challenge is to empower them by helping to establish their independence through self-directed and self-managed learning.

> *Education is life – not a preparation for life. Adolescents should be viewed as real human beings that have serious questions and concerns. Their dignity must be respected.*

(Beane, 1990, p.49)

Summary

This chapter focused extensively on the context within which learning occurs in the middle and secondary school. It highlighted the ways in which adolescents are neither child nor adult and the way in which they fit, rather uncomfortably, somewhere in the middle. Their developmental needs still vary enormously. Adolescence is a critical period of rapid, physical, emotional and intellectual development, when patterns of thinking and behaviour are established.

The chapter also explored issues related both to the journey from primary to the middle and secondary school, and to ability, attitude and achievement ranges, and curriculum and organisational structures. These factors combine to form the context of the middle and secondary school, and all have implications for pupils' learning.

3 Adolescent learners

Adolescence – between childhood and maturity

Adolescents between the ages of 10 and 16 are adjusting to profound physical, social and emotional changes. They are beginning to develop a strong sense of their own identity. They align closely with their peers, and are keen to 'belong' to the group. During this period, they are learning how to establish personal and working relationships with adults and starting to establish their own sexual identity. Adolescents can be passionate and egocentric about issues that they believe in, and their behaviour can be erratic. They fluctuate from being cynical, sullen, withdrawn and resistant one minute, to being suddenly fun-filled and gregarious the next. They are less biddable than younger children. During adolescence, pupils start to accept responsibility for making their own decisions. Although they are growing towards independence, many of them are still not self-regulating (Eyers *et al.*, 1992).

So what is different about adolescent learners?

Adolescent learners no longer think like younger children. They are conceptually more sophisticated with their learning and are able to think in ways that are progressively more abstract and reflective. They are starting to show concern about wider, contemporary issues and are trying to make sense of the social and political world beyond their own communities, especially in terms of how it affects them.

Adolescents will often challenge authority and strongly test the boundaries of adult conventions, practices and values. They are passionate about the things that interest them, and they have a tendency to become preoccupied with fashion, pop culture, and electronic and on-line games. As learners, they are at once listless and energetic, curious and bored, maddeningly obtuse and refreshingly insightful.

Adolescent learners' self-image is greatly influenced by their level of acceptance within the peer group and they afford their schools and their teachers much less importance and respect! They are keen to get 'out there' in the real world, in different learning contexts, and in different ways.

Studies of adolescent learners in Australian schools (PNS, 1996; Hill, 1993) reveal that they want to be engaged in interactive and collaborative approaches to their work. They would like their teachers to use pupil-centred teaching, learning and assessment practices, and a broader range of teaching styles and strategies than traditional teacher talk, note-taking exercises from the board, handouts and question and answer exercises. They feel they need opportunities to take on work within and beyond their school context. In other words, they would appreciate being:

> *active resources for learning, rather than passive recipients of knowledge. They believe that their knowledge, views and concerns about educational and social issues are not always recognised as being a valuable curriculum resource, and that they bring a range of diverse skills that can contribute to the learning process – as researchers, producers, peer tutors, junior sports coaches, etc.*

(Cumming, 1994a)

Whereas teachers may be hesitant to use electronic (digital) learning technologies, adolescents are seemingly at ease with experimenting and manipulating these tools. Whilst this may seem to be just a surface interest, adolescent learners often demonstrate a remarkable capacity to be innovative. They also demonstrate an ability to be fearless about experimenting with the latest technology. It is easy to dismiss adolescents' fascination with computer games, popular culture and fashion as superficial or as part of an attachment to the latest fad. It is, however, often the challenge of mastering 'new forms' or a new 'game' that provides the motivating factor. Adolescent learners respond positively to meeting these types of challenges.

Adolescents are not yet independent, and while they seem to disguise this from time to time, they are seeking acceptance as adults. Consequently, as learners, they like to negotiate their learning with teachers, and to be actively involved in all learning tasks.

Young adolescent learners are going through a rapid growth and extensive maturation phase. They need learning programmes that reflect their physical, social and emotional needs, and that help them to understand themselves. Their academic needs are also greatly affected by their physical, social and emotional needs, and these must also be addressed directly in teaching and learning programmes.

General learning principles

The characteristics of adolescent learners are not always addressed in the middle and secondary school context. Powerful learning principles can also be ignored or overlooked at this 'in between' phase of schooling.

Many statements have been made about sets of principles that facilitate learning. *First Steps*, the primary companion resource to *Stepping Out*, uses memory aids such as PEWIT and the 3R's (see p.26). *Stepping Out*, however, draws heavily from the statement of learning principles described in the Curriculum Framework for Western Australian schools. The statement (shown below) has a strong emphasis on purposeful outcomes and focused learning, and elegantly summarises contemporary understandings about effective learning:

A supportive learning environment – where pupils feel valued and challenged, and where they are able to experiment safely and work collaboratively with others.

Opportunities to learn – where pupils encounter and are engaged by their learning, and where they have opportunities to observe, practise, develop and apply new skills and understandings.

Connection and challenge – where learning links to pupils' existing knowledge and skills, and stretches them beyond what they know and can do.

Action and reflection – where pupils experience learning as an active process and use language as a tool for learning. They also get opportunities to reflect on and make sense of the action.

Motivation and purpose – where learning experiences are focused on achieving clear, relevant outcomes that make sense to them.

Inclusivity and difference – where pupils engage with experiences that respect and reflect differences between learners.

Independence and collaboration – where pupils work together, as well as individually, to ensure a personal grasp of concepts.

(Curriculum Framework, W.A., 1998)

Emphases for adolescent learners

Each one of these principles highlighted in the statement above is important. Some, however, require a particular emphasis for adolescent learners. They reflect the things that really count and if the aim is to improve learning in the middle and secondary school context, they need to be taken seriously.

Making them feel good

Adolescent learners learn more effectively when they feel good about themselves, and when they know that others like and value them. Teachers have a huge influence on pupils' self-esteem. Their perceptions, expectations and interactions can make a real difference to learning outcomes.

Minding connections

Learning is enhanced when connections are made to:
- *developmental levels*
- *existing skills, knowledge and experience*
- *family, language, cultural and socio-economic experiences*
- *different learning styles*
- *peers in the classroom*
- *learning in primary school*
- *school community members.*

Making it sing!

Subject specific content is better learned through exciting and motivating processes where learning is contextualised, relevant and where there is a strong sense of challenge.

Moving them forwards

All pupils need support to make progress with their learning. Different scaffolding is required for pupils at different levels, and for different purposes.

Making sure they're learning

There tends to be an obsession on evaluating end products in the middle and secondary school context. This takes it for granted that learning is occurring, and by that stage, it is too late to do anything to improve the <u>quality</u> of the learning that took place. Monitoring of processes and products and the collection of data over a period of time are ongoing processes that inform the teaching and learning programme. If progress is not being made, then something needs to change.

Curriculum Framework

Supportive environment

Opportunities to learn

Connection and challenge

Active engagement and reflection

Motivation and purpose

Inclusivity and difference

Independence and collaboration

Adolescent Emphases

Making them feel good

Minding the connections

Making it sing!

Moving them forwards

Making sure they're learning

First Steps

Problem solving

Embeddedness

Working memory

Interaction

Time

3R's
Reference
Representation
Reporting

Making them feel good

© 1950 by United Feature Syndicate, Inc.

The learning environment

In the rush to cover course content and to fit into the tightly organised pattern of operating in a middle or secondary school, it is easy to overlook the importance of a supportive learning environment. During adolescence, however, pupils start to question the values, beliefs, practices and conventions that they come in contact with. This is expected behaviour for this age group, but it can sometimes get them into situations of conflict! They need to work with people who let them know that they are liked and trusted, and who value their contribution. They also need to work in an environment that is conducive to forming relationships with teachers and peers – one that helps them to move safely through this particular phase of their development.

Adolescent learners need opportunities to express themselves in a 'safe' place, free from harassment, sarcasm and remarks that denigrate their input. They need to be able to 'have a go' at a wide range of things, secure in the knowledge that, while errors might be painful, lessons can always be learned from them.

Interactions and perceptions of teachers

Pupils work harder for teachers who notice their efforts. They also remember the teachers who made them feel that they were a valuable member of the class.

> *Good teachers are those we can talk to – who are understanding and show respect for people with different ideas ... who are interested in us as individuals.*

(Pupil, SA Field Study, 1994)

Some teachers strongly believe that their teaching methods and strategies significantly affect the learning outcomes of their pupils. This belief reflects an *internal locus of control*. Other teachers do not share this belief and attribute pupils' successes and failures in the classroom to things beyond their own control, such as pupils' intelligence levels, attitudes, levels of motivation and home backgrounds. This belief reflects an *external locus of control*.

A study of over 300 Australian teachers found that a large majority (62%) attributed learning problems to factors within pupils (i.e. limited intellectual ability, or poor concentration span, deficient memory processes, restricted vocabulary, sensory impairments, lack of interest, low motivation, negative attitudes, bad behaviour, laziness, hyperactivity, and learned helplessness).

A significant number (14%) of the teachers attributed pupils' learning problems to factors related to family background culture (non-English speaking background, low literacy levels in parents, single parent family, poor home management). Only 10% of the comments reflected an awareness of the fact that curriculum content and teaching methods can cause pupils to have learning problems.

Within the pupil **62%**	*Within the family background or culture* **14%**	*Within the peer group* **3%**
Within the curriculum **8%**	*Within the teaching approach* **2%**	*Within the pupil/ teacher relationship* **4%**
Within the school/ classroom environment **6%**	*Other* **1%**	

The above diagram reflects the tendency to *overestimate* the contribution of factors within the learner, and to *underestimate* the powerful influences of teaching methods and the school curriculum. Yet the variable over which teachers have most control is the way in which they teach.

In contrast to these beliefs, research has demonstrated consistently that teachers' attitudes and opinions have a significant influence on pupils' success at school. When teachers believe that a particular pupil cannot achieve, that pupil's performance can be influenced in negative ways. When teachers believe that a particular pupil can achieve, the pupil's performance is influenced in positive ways. This phenomenon, called the 'self-fulfilling prophecy', suggests that pupils become 'what they are expected to become'.

> *The most effective strategy for dealing with learning problems is to improve the quality of instruction.*
>
> (Ginsburg, 1989, p.237 cited in Westwood, 1995, p.21)

When teachers expect good things from pupils, they tend to:

- interact and react warmly to them
- provide more feedback about their performance
- encourage their efforts more
- teach them more difficult material
- give them more opportunities to respond and question.

Adolescents quickly notice what each teacher will accept. They will (quite happily) provide work of a higher standard for the teacher who expects it, and work of a much lower standard for another teacher. When high standards are expected, and explicit and encouraging feedback is provided, they feel that the extra effort they put into their work is important, noticed and valued. It makes them feel good about themselves.

Minding the connections

Learning programmes for adolescents require teachers to connect to, and challenge, what pupils already know and can do. This involves *connecting to*, *recruiting*, *building on* and *stretching* what pupils know. These processes are critical elements of any learning programme. The connections need to be made at a variety of levels.

Connecting to developmental levels

Adolescent learners develop and learn in different ways. *What* they learn, *how* they learn, the *rate* at which they learn and the *order* in which they learn are shaped by the social contexts within which they interact. Typically, they go through stages as they develop in an area of learning, and the characteristics they demonstrate at each stage can be different from that at every other stage. It is unrealistic to expect them to be successful at tasks that require a level of cognitive ability not yet attained. If they are not ready to take on the learning, these tasks can set pupils up to fail.

The implications for developmental learning theory are that teachers need to know each pupil's stage of development, so that appropriate learning strategies and activities can be incorporated at the point of need.

Connecting to and extending existing knowledge, skills and experience

All pupils have existing knowledge, skills, understandings and experiences. These need to be identified, *linked* to, and/or *recruited* as a curriculum resource. Once teachers have identified what pupils know about a concept or topic and what skills or experiences they can contribute to the curriculum, they can plan programmes that bridge the gap (lessen the distance) between what is already known and what is to be learned.

Many strategies can be used at the start of a unit of work, a concept, or topic lesson to identify what pupils already know. These strategies enable pupils to use and hear subject specific vocabulary and to reinforce and extend their knowledge as they talk, listen and piggy-back ideas off each other. *Journal writing* or *concept maps* provide a wealth of information about what pupils know. *Anticipation or prediction activities* are useful to implement at the start of a new topic, because they encourage pupils to think about what a topic might cover. Their initial predictions can be referred to, compared and contrasted and/or amended at different stages of the unit of work. Similarly, simple strategies like a *quick quiz*, when repeated at different stages of a unit of work, make it clear that scores increase as knowledge about a topic increases. The comparisons enable everyone to see how much learning has occurred!

New learning occurs when thinking is challenged and extended. Adolescent learners need to be *stretched* (with assistance) from the edge of what they can do independently to the next point of their learning. As they are *stretched*, they start to build up new knowledge, understandings and skills. Simple strategies, such as *three level guides*, *directed silent reading*, and *pupil generated questions*, can be used to move pupils along from surface levels of reading and research to more advanced levels of thinking, research and application. (Several of the suggested strategies are described in the *Stepping Out* programme.)

Connecting to family, language, cultural and socio-economic experiences

The experiences that pupils bring to school with them are often referred to as background experiences, because they are not related to the business of schooling. The experiences are central to adolescent learners' identities, and they don't disappear while they are at school. Not only do learning programmes need to *link to* these experiences, they also need to *recruit* them in such a way that they are put into the foreground of all learning activities.

> *All the things we bring to the learning situation – our language, previous learning, family and cultural background, and our experiences – are the pegs on which we hang new information. If we can't attach new information to what we know already, we can't learn it ... it's as simple as that.*

(Lingo video, 1992)

Connecting to learning across subject areas

Pupils' learning outcomes improve when they are able to make links across different learning areas. Teachers have to help them to make these links, but they can only do this if they work collaboratively, sharing ideas and seeing themselves as part of a team responsible for the development of all the pupils in the school.

It may be easy for some schools to become more collaborative about they way in which they work. However, for many teachers and for many schools, the issues require a great deal of patience and effort and are not easy to address. Improving how schools work is something valuable to target, but it tends to happen over time. Whilst the efforts of individuals, departments and key stakeholders are essential to achieving such reform, it is not likely to happen immediately. In the meantime, teachers have to work within their existing school culture and organisation to avoid fragmentation, duplication and overlap, and to effect improvement in learning.

Many schools have tried different ways of organising the learning environment to cater for the needs of adolescent learners. They have clustered pupils in various primary/secondary configurations, set up sub-schools and teaching/learning teams (thus creating communities of learners), reduced the number of teachers that pupils encounter, made the timetable more flexible by ensuring larger, uninterrupted blocks of time for learning, and integrated the curriculum.

Some schools continue consistently to examine their current practice to identify how their organisational structures and timetabling processes impact on pupils' learning. They collect data to inform the planning and implementing of strategies that minimise barriers to learning. They use this type of analysis to identify options and possibilities for engaging pupils in their own learning and for giving them responsibility for making decisions about their own learning programmes.

Murphy (1997) suggests a range of solutions for finding an hour per week to do some collaborative planning. Permission from a range of sources may be needed for some suggestions.

- Release pupils one day per week, at an earlier time.
- Start school 30 minutes later than the regular starting time one day a week – but ask teachers to arrive 30 minutes earlier than the usual starting time.
- Timetable pupils to attend art, music, physical education, and arrange for a group of teachers to meet at this time, while specialist teachers work with their pupils.
- Hire a small group of relief teachers one day per fortnight. These teachers enable five teachers to meet at a time, for one hour periods, over the course of a day.
- Limit learning area meeting to one afternoon per month, and use the other weekly meetings as planning meetings.

Connecting to different learning styles

All learners have preferred learning and working styles. They might have certain approaches in common, but they generally retain preferences that are uniquely their own. These different learning styles need to be *linked* and *recruited* into all aspects of the curriculum. Kinaesthetic (tactile) learners, who make up the vast majority of the drop-out rate in secondary schools, cannot sit still for long periods of time and need to *move* and *touch* things in order to demonstrate their learning effectively. They are unlikely to do well in tests and programmes that reinforce a narrow range of learning styles. Individual differences are important and need to be recognised and respected when planning learning programmes.

On the other hand, adolescents can be *challenged and stretched* when they are expected to demonstrate their learning in different ways (i.e. through drama, art, graphs, diagrams, music, dance, etc.). They learn to accommodate and appreciate other pupils' ways of working when they participate in collaborative small group work. Some pupils do not necessarily work well in groups, and consideration needs to be given to those who work best alone. Group activities that start with 10–15 minutes of individual thinking or planning time (or build in individual reflection time incorporated at various stages of the learning programme) can provide successful learning opportunities for all pupils.

Different learning styles can be accommodated by:

- encouraging *team teaching* within a subject department or school (so that pupils are exposed to a range of teaching styles)
- utilising *small group work*, such as *jigsaw activities*, that allow pupils to use their strengths when contributing to group tasks
- taking an area of curriculum and developing *thematic units* that accommodate pupils' various learning styles
- providing a balanced range of activities that incorporate elements of individual, small group or whole class learning.

Connecting to other pupils

Adolescent learners learn about the world and generate, test out, refine and extend their ideas through talk. They learn best when they can work with their peers in pairs or groups of three or four. Small group activities provide ideal opportunities for this *linking* and *recruiting* of ideas to happen.

Connecting to learning in primary schools

The National Literacy Strategy highlights the importance of *linking to* and *recruiting* the ideas, perceptions and information of primary teachers who have already taught the same pupils. Much is to be gained when the strengths and knowledge of primary pedagogy and secondary subject specific expertise is shared. In particular, the sharing of information about curriculum and pedagogy might also overcome the findings of Rudduck, Chaplain and Wallace (1996).

> *Year 7 work is not too difficult – it's more or less the same as Year 6. I've been asked to draw round six leaves (yet) I did photosynthesis in my last school and I'm interested in what effect different light might have on its rate.*

Connecting to others in the school community

Pupil, teacher, family and community partnerships provide powerful links for pupil learning. Learning opportunities are enhanced when a school community *links to, recruits and extends* the expertise, skills, support, cultural experiences, resources, facilities, business acumen and knowledge of its members, and when all are engaged in meaningful, proactive ways.

Schools should no longer be seen as the primary producers, delivers and assessors of knowledge and skills. Pupils need a broader education that will enable them to participate in, and also contribute to, society. Community-based learning is learning that takes place in the community, beyond the confines of the classroom and the school. It involves individuals, other than teachers, as part of the learning process. Pupils remain at the centre of the learning process, while maintaining connections to, and support from, teachers, parents and other community members.

The emphasis is on co-operative planning, implementation and evaluation of meaningful and productive work that has a strong educational focus, and clearly articulated outcomes. Pupils participate in activities that are real, rather than simulated, and the results of their work can be exhibited, presented and acknowledged in community settings.

Making it sing!

Balancing content and processes

Just at a time when motivational, purposeful and challenging learning experiences are most needed, adolescent learners become flooded with information and have to scurry through copious amounts of subject specific content. Middle and secondary school teachers, faced with an array of pupil groups, challenging behaviours and demands for course coverage, can easily be tempted to play it safe by restricting the pedagogy, narrowing the curriculum design and limiting the degree of interaction. At the point where language demands are at their greatest, opportunities for pupils to practise using language as a learning tool are often minimised.

For adolescent learners, the first flush of enthusiasm and successful learning experiences often seem to have happened a long while ago. And the finishing line for the schooling journey still seems a long way ahead. As an alienated, bored pupil in one study commented:

> *All these boring worksheets … the answers come ten minutes later anyway, so why do them?*

(Rudduck, Chaplain and Wallace, 1996)

The emphasis on 'making it sing' means more than simply making learning fun. It also means more than simply covering content. 'Making it sing' means involving and incorporating the other *Stepping Out* emphases. In particular, it means designing learning experiences that balance the demands between process and content outcomes. Many middle and secondary teachers comment that there is too much content to deliver in too little time and have pointed out the similarities between driving sheep through a gate, and moving pupils through a mass of curriculum content. Content is important, but it is just as important to remember that much of what is taught today might well be irrelevant or superseded in a few years' time. Pupils complain that they spend far too much time learning about things that they don't believe will ever be useful to them. What really matters, and what is important, is that they are equipped with transportable tools for learning that can be applied to any body of content.

Simply 'covering' or teaching a topic does not guarantee that learning has occurred. Pupils learn best when they are given time to process and absorb or internalise the information. They need time to listen, read, think, talk, plan, write and reflect on and represent their understandings – independently, and with others. Once they have internalised the information, they can then apply or translate it to other contexts.

So processes matter, because they impact on the effectiveness and on the quality of the learning, and they require time. Striking a balance between the need for teachers to 'deliver' content and for pupils to process information will continue to be an ongoing issue in the middle and secondary school context.

It is assessment which helps us distinguish between teaching and learning.

Bud Blake (Courtesy King Features Syndicate Inc)
Geoff Coleman and Peter Cole

As part of a solution to this issue, some schools have found it useful to conduct a subject or school audit of what is taught at each year level. They determined what content was mandated and was therefore non-negotiable, and they identified what content could be compacted or removed. They examined what was happening across the school, to ensure that content was not being repeated, and in doing so, determined that responsibility for teaching a particular concept could be shared between teachers from different subject areas.

Some schools have trialled team teaching as an option for teaching a topic, concept, theme or unit of work. Others have developed integrated learning programmes with teachers from another subject area. They started small, and trialled their efforts. Successful programmes were shared within and across schools, and pupils' work samples have been used as exemplary models for others.

Contextualising the learning

When learning is contextualised, it becomes meaningful. Adolescent learners love to learn real things. They want to be part of life in the real world. They like to be 'out there' doing things that they deem to be important, and things that link to their own experiences. The more direct or 'hands on' the experience, the better. If the 'real thing' is not an option, then indirect, vicarious or simulated experiences also allow them to feel that they are close to the action. These kinds of experiences provide a context within which learning can occur, and a shared experience that can be used as a stimulus for language and knowledge extension and enrichment.

Adolescent learners like to know *why* and *how* information learned at school will be useful to them. When they know why the information is being taught, how it fits into the bigger world, and how it links to their own life, they are more likely to take the learning on board.

When learning takes place in contexts outside the classroom (in the workplace, a church, museum or shopping centre), pupils are able to observe ways of behaving, ways of speaking and conventions that are particular to certain situations. They quickly learn to adapt their own language and behaviour according to purpose and audience. Learning that occurs 'on site' can be more meaningful than learning conducted in an isolated classroom, away from the real action.

Many pupils need to explore, discuss, mind-map, brainstorm or research a topic before they are able to write about it effectively. These types of *before* activities prepare pupils for the work that is to follow. They provide the background information and content that pupils can write about.

Calvin and Hobbes cartoons, by Bill Waterson, are reproduced by permission of International Press

Pupils are also more likely to write, perform and design well if they see the processes involved in writing, designing, organising and performing modelled, and if they encounter examples of good writing, designing, organising and performing. When they encounter high quality products of those processes, they can see what it is they are aiming for.

Keeping it relevant, engaging and motivational

Adolescent learners like to be part of what is current or topical. Classroom programmes that utilise media, television, CD Roms, videos, and other forms of digital and learning technologies are more likely to engage pupils' interest. When the learning programme incorporates, links to, recruits or extends current issues, human interest stories, politics, or nuclear energy concerns, pupils are able to build up knowledge about the one topic from a range of sources. Topical news broadcasts, feature articles, films, comic strips, or the community and daily newspaper can become rich and motivating sources of topics for discussion, debate or research.

Pupils can listen, talk, read, write, think critically – often without being aware that they are learning, because they become so engrossed in the task or topic at hand. When teachers know their pupils well, they are able to tap into what is of interest at the time, and use this interest as the basis for learning.

Rapid changes in technology mean that pupils can locate information from across the world, via fax, e-mail, chat rooms, bulletin boards and so on – how much better to be able to ask pupils in other countries or contexts direct questions about their life, to be able to make contact with a real nuclear scientist or renowned explorer by fax or e-mail. The world becomes a smaller place when access is only minutes away.

Adolescent learners enjoy working collaboratively in small group activities. Debating, in particular, is an excellent strategy for engaging pupils in purposeful, relevant and motivational learning. It requires research work, planning and preparation, time keeping skills, formal language and a requirement to fit to a recognised convention, and also enables them to practise speaking at length on any given topic, in public.

Similarly, collaborative activities such as writing to the community paper about a local issue, the creation of board games, rewriting a chapter of a subject specific book in 'pupil friendly' terms, setting up worm farms or a school environmental centre, developing a powerpoint or multimedia presentation advertising the school, rewriting a chapter of a maths text for younger pupils, designing a local shopping centre or a solar car, writing and presenting a play on a health issue, writing a restaurant review after visiting the nearby Thai restaurant, designing a school Web page, designing a playground for the local nursery school, making up subject specific lyrics to a well-known song, creating quizzes and competitions, setting up a school radio station, developing a group picture book on a subject specific topic, or constructing a newspaper for a particular audience are all pupil-centred activities that provide a motivating stimulus for learning.

Integrated programmes that incorporate content from two or three subject areas are excellent vehicles for meaningful, pupil-centred learning. Issues relating to maintaining the integrity of the different subjects can be solved by ensuring that the learning is planned (and taught) collaboratively, that pupils are aware of where particular subject area concepts have been incorporated, that dedicated teaching time for each subject is planned for, and that learning programmes are analysed at the end of the unit, to identify subject components within the course of study.

Adolescent pupils relish autonomy, and become energised when the goals for learning are self-determined or negotiated, when the research topics to be interrogated are of interest to them, when they are given real problems to solve and when they are able jointly to negotiate the assessment regime. They enjoy planning and working independently, and working collaboratively with others. They also thrive on being able to be active, independent and self-directed in their approaches to learning tasks. When reflection time is built into all learning activities, their learning is even more enhanced. Teachers reinforce the message that they have trust in their pupils' ability when they are prepared to act as facilitators for learning, rather than always being the 'one who knows'.

> *The spin-offs from student participation in curriculum are many, and schools here are only beginning to understand the immense resource that is made available when students' energy and interest is used constructively for their own and one another's benefit.*

> (Brennan and Sachs, 1998, p.16)

Setting horizons

Adolescent learners need clear and achievable outcomes to strive for. They need them for each unit of work, and for each lesson. They need to know *what* they have to do, *why* they are doing it and *how* they will be doing it. Setting a purpose is similar to deciding on a destination. Unless they know where they are going, the journey is likely to be somewhat aimless. The purpose has to be worthwhile, or relevant, just as the final destination of a trip has to have been worth the effort of getting there. For each learning sequence and lesson, communicating what is to be achieved is therefore a prime requirement.

Adolescent learners are more sophisticated and are more likely to be committed to programmes that allow them some autonomy. They enjoy planning, organising, implementing and evaluating activities and learning that has been negotiated with their teachers. The degree of negotiations might range from a single task within a programme, to complete freedom of choice, depending on pupils' needs, abilities and interests, and depending on what feels comfortable for the teacher. Their self-esteem is raised when teachers indicate that they are confident in their ability to manage aspects of their own learning.

Whilst it may seem a paradox, adolescents and learners need both the challenge of working under pressure to achieve high standards and time to reflect so that new and difficult concepts can be refined and internalised. It is also at this stage in their development that adolescents become more self-aware learners, and need to be challenged to 'think about their thinking'.

Moving them forwards

The middle and lower secondary phase of schooling is often regarded as being rather 'aimless' because it falls in between the phases of schooling that are considered to really matter. As an antidote to this, it is important that pupils recognise that they are making progress with their learning. The key issue is to support their learning without losing sight of the necessity to develop independent learners.

Supporting learning All learners require support (or scaffolding) to move from one level to the next (from *what they know* to *what they need to know next*). The characteristics they demonstrate at each level provide a basis for deciding what strategies need to be put in place to support them to make further progress towards target attainment levels or outcomes. The strategies need to be appropriate both for adolescent pupils and to their developmental level.

Even pupils who demonstrate high learning outcomes need to have support. Those, for instance, who demonstrate outstanding computer skills still require support to continue to make progress, whereas those starting to experiment with a computer keyboard need support of a different kind. Pupils, adults or teachers can provide this type of support at the different points that lead to the mastery of a concept or skill. It is not necessary to provide the same support at the whole class level unless, of course, the whole class is learning a new skill at the same time.

It is important to know that the majority of adolescent learners prefer to fade into the background – they are not always receptive to having their peers observe them 'being helped'. Sometimes it is more discreet to offer support at the small group level, so that individual pupils do not feel conspicuous.

Adolescent learners need the support of scaffolding strategies to *stretch* to the next phase of their learning. The use of trainer wheels on a bicycle is an example of scaffolding. Trainer wheels are used until the cyclist practises riding the bicycle independently, becoming more confident as he or she experiences success. When the wheels are removed, it is a sign that learning has taken place, and is a mark of progress.

Scaffolding does not stay in place forever! It should be removed once it is no longer needed, or replaced by a different support strategy when necessary. This gradual release of scaffolding places the final responsibility for learning on the pupil.

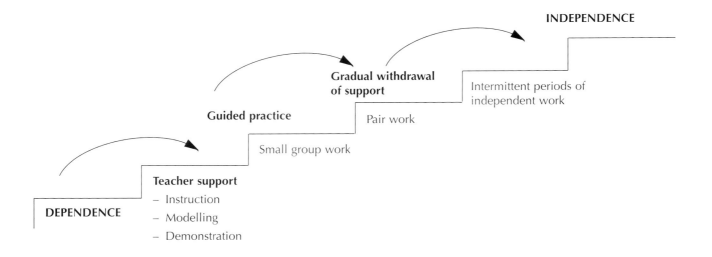

> *Scaffolding needs to happen recursively with each new concept or task that pupils are asked to consider.*

When teachers know how different strategies work, and where they can be used effectively, they are able confidently to select those that will provide the most appropriate support for a task. When selecting scaffolding strategies, it is important to determine:

– who needs support
– what kind of support would be most appropriate
– how long the support is needed for
– when to remove or vary the supportive scaffolding.

Types of scaffolding can vary, but generally include strategies such as these:

Immersion (Familiarisation)	Models or examples are provided, so that pupils become familiar with, and can identify, common patterns, structures or features of a text.
Explicit Teaching and Feedback	The teacher explicitly explains the steps involved in a task and provides ongoing feedback as pupils 'approximate' the task.
Modelling and Demonstrating	The teacher demonstrates a process whilst 'thinking aloud', so that pupils see how others tackle a task, and also 'hear the thinking' that leads to the completion of the task.
Guided Reading or Viewing	The teacher uses strategies such as focus questions or note-making frameworks or viewing at *before, during* and *after* stages of the reading task. These help pupils to 'navigate' their way through the task.
Guided Writing	The teacher supports individuals, pairs or groups of pupils as they tentatively compose a piece of writing. Strategies such as explicit teaching, peer evaluation or writing frameworks are used at the point of need.
Joint Construction	The teacher and pupils share ideas and jointly construct a written genre, a note-making framework, graphs or diagrams. The overhead projector or board can be used.

Teachers frequently make the majority of decisions about tasks to be completed in class, selecting strategies, activities and evaluation methods. This often means that valuable opportunities where pupils could use thinking skills to determine which writing framework or note-making structure might be more appropriate, to practise the skills involved in selecting appropriate strategies for particular tasks, to develop the skills of time management, and to develop the skills required to be independent, self-regulating learners are lost.

When teachers make all the decisions about what is to happen in the classroom, pupils are denied valuable opportunities to make confident, informed choices about the purpose and appropriateness of different strategies for particular activities. They can get used to being 'spoon-fed', and quickly become dependent learners (Kiddey, 1998). On the other hand, some pupils simply do not have the developmental, organisational or self-management skills required to complete their work independently. They cannot be left to take responsibility for managing their learning, because their learning needs to be supported. There is a fine line, then, between knowing *who* to support, *when* to support and *how* to support pupils' learning, and *when to wean them off* the support. The only way that teachers can effectively gauge how pupils are progressing with their learning is to monitor them as they work on processes over a period of time, in a range of different contexts.

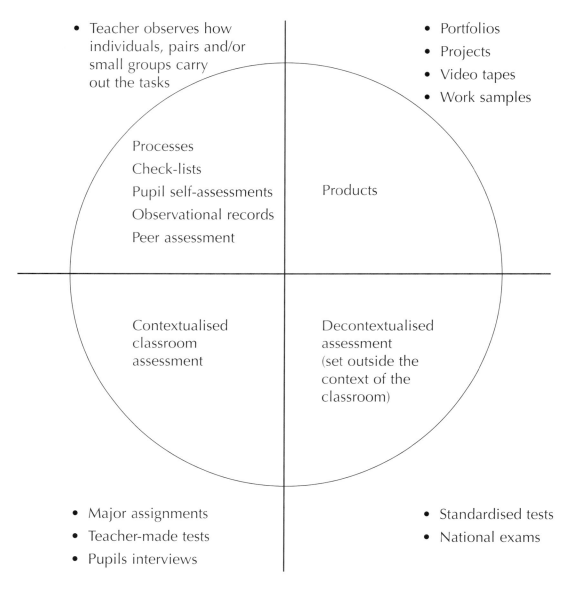

- Teacher observes how individuals, pairs and/or small groups carry out the tasks

- Portfolios
- Projects
- Video tapes
- Work samples

Processes
Check-lists
Pupil self-assessments
Observational records
Peer assessment

Products

Contextualised classroom assessment

Decontextualised assessment (set outside the context of the classroom)

- Major assignments
- Teacher-made tests
- Pupils interviews

- Standardised tests
- National exams

Adapted from Anthony, Johnson, Mickleson and Preece (1991), *Evaluating Literacy – A Perspective for Change*, Rigby Heinemann, Australia.

Making sure they're learning

If the prime responsibility of teachers 'is not to teach but to ensure that students learn' (Dimmock, 1993), then the prime purpose of assessment is to ensure that learning has taken place. Teachers need to know what their pupils know and can do, in relation to target learning outcomes. They are then able to put in place a learning programme that will enable pupils to make further progress. An additional purpose of assessment is to be able to report on pupil competence and achievement.

Assessment

Assessment of pupil performance allows for judgements to be made about the levels of competence they have reached. The principles that apply for learning and teaching and the learning emphases for adolescents also apply directly to assessment. Over the past ten years, with the increased focus on the importance of assessment and the advent of resources such as *First Steps,* there has been a stronger emphasis on integrating assessment, learning and teaching. The middle and secondary years have not been so amenable to these developments.

What adolescent learners face

As pupils make the transition from primary school to middle or secondary school, the stark differences experienced in curriculum, pedagogy and organisation carry over into the assessment regime they face. Part of the transition experience is an increase in the seriousness with which the community regards the business of schooling. The process of sifting and sorting pupils for further phases of education and for life beyond schools starts in earnest in early secondary school.

As a consequence, the assessment policies and practices of most middle and secondary schools, and the formality and weight put on the reliability of assessments, reflect this increase in seriousness.

Adolescent learners are faced with a diet of frequent, content-focused testing within each subject area, the advent of formal 'exams' in senior schools, and a much stronger emphasis on formal expository writing. The purpose of the assessment process shifts to a preoccupation with the allocation of grades or levels. This information often starts to count towards the 'external' purpose of assessment, to meet requirements for access to subjects in senior secondary years, or for certification. There is much more of a feeling in the middle and secondary context that assessment is something which is 'done' to pupils. The assessment tasks that pupils face are not always relevant, and the literacy demands of some assessment tasks often, unwittingly, set some pupils up to fail.

Assessment issues

It is not an easy task for middle and secondary schools to develop assessment regimes which can cope effectively with the mounting pressures placed on them. All too often the compromise is weighted toward responding to the external pressures, at the expense of the needs of adolescent learners. Some of the issues that middle and secondary schools must address include the following:

Over-assessment – There is a tendency to over-assess pupils in middle/lower secondary school to cope with the increasing demands of the curriculum and to supply information for accountability purposes.

Narrow range – While there is a great deal of assessment going on, much of it is narrow in focus and is concentrated on measuring whether pupils have acquired course content.

Lack of integration – Much of the assessment is summative and can be regarded as being tacked on to learning and teaching, rather than being an integral part of it.

Pupil numbers and specialisation – Teachers in primary schools get to know their pupils well and are able to collect rich diagnostic information. The sheer weight of pupil numbers that secondary teachers have responsibility for and the limited time they see them make the use of devices such as developmental continuums problematical. Middle and secondary teachers feel snowed under when they are given a large amount of information that they cannot use effectively.

Improving the assessment regime

Cartoon courtesy of Deborah Fullwood

The regime typically encountered by adolescents in the middle and secondary school tends to be formal, and does not always match well with their learning characteristics, or with the teaching and learning emphases required for this group of learners. The literacy demands of some assessment tasks can, unwittingly, set pupils up to fail. Some ways of improving the assessment regime might include the following:

Variety and range of assessments – If learning experiences are to be varied and challenging, so also must the assessment! An expanded range of broad, well-designed assessment tasks should provide opportunities for observation and assessment of performance, and the collection of hard and soft data for individual and group work. These should reflect the spread of needs and interests of pupils in each classroom. *Open-ended tasks* that incorporate multiple entry points allow pupils to demonstrate higher levels of understandings that may not have been predicted. The *integration* of assessment tasks at various points within the learning programme ensures that teaching is able to be targeted at points of need.

Purposeful assessment in 'real' contexts – Adolescents are less accepting of the ritual of formal assessment. As a consequence, the assessment regime needs to be ongoing, and to monitor pupils' learning outcomes in contexts that are perceived to be 'lifelike'. Where pupils take a long time to move from one large and significant level to the next, teachers need to use fine-grained information to indicate that small, incremental steps of progress are, in fact, being made.

Kid watching

Most teachers know a great deal of information about their pupils' learning. They gain a rich source of information about their behaviour, performance, strengths and weaknesses through 'kid watching' (Goodman, 1985), as they observe pupils working on tasks, in a range of contexts and over a period of time. This information can be recorded – on informal *running records*, a *retrieval chart* or against a *check-list of criteria*. 'On balance' judgements should take into account the relative weight of the evidence collected. The range of assessment methods that teachers use can include the following:

Pupil portfolios, which connect separate items of a pupil's work to form clearer and fuller pictures of each pupil as a learner (EDWA, 1999). They are a valid and reliable source of evidence for making judgements about pupil achievement. They show pupils' ability to apply their skills in a range of situations. Portfolios can be used to demonstrate evidence that incremental steps of progress are being made. They can be used in one learning area, or can include work across a range of learning areas.

INSIDE A PORTFOLIO

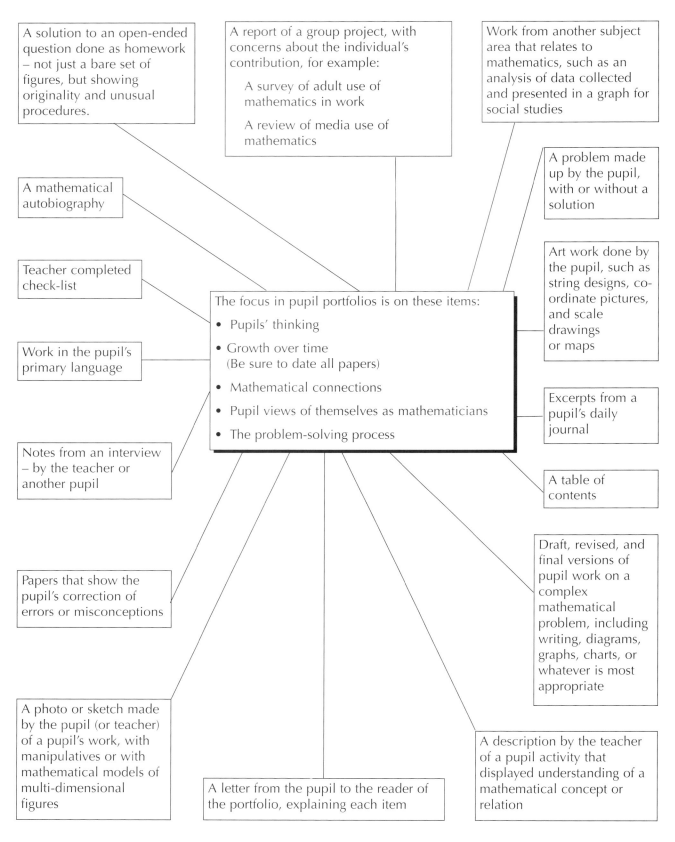

A solution to an open-ended question done as homework – not just a bare set of figures, but showing originality and unusual procedures.

A report of a group project, with concerns about the individual's contribution, for example:

A survey of adult use of mathematics in work

A review of media use of mathematics

Work from another subject area that relates to mathematics, such as an analysis of data collected and presented in a graph for social studies

A mathematical autobiography

Teacher completed check-list

Work in the pupil's primary language

Notes from an interview – by the teacher or another pupil

The focus in pupil portfolios is on these items:

- Pupils' thinking
- Growth over time (Be sure to date all papers)
- Mathematical connections
- Pupil views of themselves as mathematicians
- The problem-solving process

A problem made up by the pupil, with or without a solution

Art work done by the pupil, such as string designs, co-ordinate pictures, and scale drawings or maps

Excerpts from a pupil's daily journal

A table of contents

Papers that show the pupil's correction of errors or misconceptions

Draft, revised, and final versions of pupil work on a complex mathematical problem, including writing, diagrams, graphs, charts, or whatever is most appropriate

A photo or sketch made by the pupil (or teacher) of a pupil's work, with manipulatives or with mathematical models of multi-dimensional figures

A letter from the pupil to the reader of the portfolio, explaining each item

A description by the teacher of a pupil activity that displayed understanding of a mathematical concept or relation

Taken from Stenmark, J. (1991, p.37)

Different types of portfolio serve different purposes:

Working portfolios, that contain sketches, notes, half-finished drafts and completed work. These provide an interactive context for ongoing instruction and feedback.

Documentary portfolios, that contain collections of pupils' work assembled specifically for assessment. They contain not only final products of pupil work, but also evidence of the processes that pupils use to develop these products.

Show portfolios, that contain selections of materials designed to reflect the best of pupil work. These can be used for certification, as well as classroom assessment.

Portfolio assessment is a process that provides visible evidence that pupils are making progress. They are particularly useful for pupils who need a longer time to move from one level to the next, because fine-grained evidence of achievement, including teacher observations, check-lists, pupil drafts, journal writing examples, self and peer evaluation sheets, audio and video tapes of pupil work, and so on can be included. The criteria for portfolio assessment should alter as tasks, demands and pupil understandings change. Purpose statements and 'road maps' or guides can lead the reader through the portfolio. Captions or statements attached to each document are also helpful, because these can describe what the document is, why it has been included, and what learning outcomes it demonstrates. They also require summaries or final reflective statements, to summarise documents in the portfolio and to articulate what has been learned (Masters and Forster, 1996).

Some issues that would need to be clarified at the whole school level would include determining:

- the purpose for implementing portfolio assessment
- which teacher(s) (or which learning area(s)) will trial the use of portfolios – and over what period of time
- how parents will be notified of the move towards portfolio assessment
- the purpose of the portfolios
- the range of samples within the portfolios
- logistics related to storage
- whether the portfolios will remain at school and be handed to pupils' new teacher each year – or whether they will be sent home at the end of each year
- the target audience for portfolios
- the balance between pupil self-selection of samples and teacher nominated pieces
- ways in which portfolios would be reported on
- times when portfolios would be sent home for parent feedback
- the importance of planning for organisational time, so that pupils can sort, select, and incorporate samples in their portfolio
- ways in which pupils who require additional support to build up their portfolio can be assisted.

Portfolios serve different purposes as pupils move towards becoming independent learners. Examples of such purposes are outlined in the following diagram.

Year group	Purpose of portfolio	Audience for portfolio
Year 7	<ul><li>To demonstrate the learning process</li><li>To develop skills of reflection and self-evaluation</li><li>To encourage goal-setting</li><li>As a means of communicating with parents</li><li>To demonstrate achievement</li></ul>	Pupils Parents Other schools
Year 8	<ul><li>To demonstrate the learning process</li><li>To develop skills of reflection and self-evaluation</li><li>To encourage goal-setting</li><li>As a means of communicating with parents</li><li>To demonstrate achievement</li></ul>	Pupils Parents
Year 9	<ul><li>To demonstrate the learning process</li><li>To develop skills of reflection and self-evaluation including realistically evaluating own strengths and interests in terms of future subject and study path choices</li><li>To encourage goal-setting with longer term goals becoming more significant</li><li>As a means of communicating with parents</li><li>As a means of collecting documentation which will be useful in career/education placing</li><li>To demonstrate achievement</li></ul>	Pupils Parents
Year 10	<ul><li>As a means of collecting samples of best work produced in each Learning Area</li><li>As a means of collecting documentation which will be useful in career planning and in interviews</li><li>To set goals, both long and short term</li><li>To facilitate reflection and self-evaluation</li><li>Communication with parents</li><li>As a means of demonstrating achievement</li></ul>	Employers Further study institutions Career advisers Parents Pupil
Year 11	<ul><li>To demonstrate best work in all subjects studied</li><li>To collect documentation for career planning and for interviews</li><li>To facilitate reflection and self-evaluation</li><li>Goal-setting, particularly long term</li><li>Communication with parents</li><li>As a means of demonstrating achievement</li></ul>	Employers Further study institutions Parents Pupil

Taken from Ballajura Community College, 1998.

Teachers need to know what their pupils know and can do in relation to target learning outcomes. They are then able to put in place a learning programme that incorporates strategies that will enable pupils to make progress.

Other types of assessment

Peer assessment, encourages pupils to make decisions about their peers' performance, based on explicit, jointly negotiated or predetermined criteria.

Pupil/teacher conferences involve pupil and teacher in joint negotiations about performance and follow-up action.

Performance assessment focuses on pupils' performances or products which are used to demonstrate the degree to which pupils can apply and demonstrate their learning.

Tests measure a sample of pupil performance at a particular point in time under standardised conditions. It is important to keep in mind that traditional testing methods are useful, but that they can be narrow in scope, and do not always allow pupils to demonstrate a wide range of skills. You do not always allow for different learning styles or unexpected resources.

Projects, reports and assignments encourage pupils to engage in the class and/or out of class research activities.

Open-ended assessment tasks provide different entry points and different points of assessment integrated within the task. Teaching can be targeted at the point of need, as pupils can work at their own rate and at their own level of ability. Open-ended tasks are problem solving tasks. They provide opportunities for pupils to demonstrate their skills and knowledge, to apply their different learning styles and to demonstrate different learning outcomes. They also provide opportunities for developing and refining creative and problem solving skills.

Assessment criteria for open-ended tasks need to cater for a range of levels. The criteria do not always have to be decided in advance. Pupils will often demonstrate higher levels of understanding or outcomes that were not envisaged as being part of the task. These can be recorded for future reference.

Marking keys are also beneficial. Pupils perform better when they know and understand the criteria that will be used for assessment and evaluation. When goals and assessments are known in advance, the results reflect what *pupils know* and *can do*, as opposed to reflecting how well pupils anticipate what would be contained in the test.

Marking keys help teachers to:

— set clear guidelines
— assess content objectives and pupil outcomes
— provide detailed feedback
— assist pupils to improve on previous work.

Marking keys help pupils to:

— stay on task
— know what the teacher wants
— improve on previous work.

Marking Key for Interviewing

TOPIC: _____ DATE: _____

NAME OF INTERVIEWER: _____ NAME OF INTERVIEWEE: _____

A Matter – 4 marks	**A Matter – 4 marks**
1. Good evidence of research displayed. ☐	1. Sufficient evidence of research displayed. ☐
2. Effective open-ended questions constructed. ☐	2. Demonstrates a good understanding of topic/issues. ☐
3. Questions display a good understanding of issues/topic. ☐	3. Ideas well supported, with appropriate examples and details. ☐
4. Evidence of active listening Construction of questions arising from comments made by interviewee. ☐	4. Reasons effectively answered the questions asked. ☐
B Manner – 4 marks ☐	**B Manner – 4 marks** ☐
1. Confident manner.	1. Answers questions confidently.
2. Speaks clearly and audibly. ☐	2. Speaks clearly and audibly. ☐
3. Gives appropriate body messages to interviewee. ☐	3. Gives appropriate body messages to interviewer. ☐
4. Pace of delivery is appropriate. ☐	4. Pace of delivery is appropriate. ☐
C Method (Structure) – 2 marks	**C Method (Structure) – 2 marks**
1. Interview contained a clear introduction. ☐	1. Answers ordered in a logical fashion. ☐
2. Questions asked in a logical order. ☐	2. Answers kept to the point, with the most important ideas addressed. ☐
TOTAL: ☐	TOTAL: ☐

Adjudicator: _____

Marking Key for Debating in Science

YEAR: _____ CLASS: _____

TOPIC: _____ DATE: _____

	AFFIRMATIVE			NEGATIVE		
	1st	2nd	3rd	1st	2nd	3rd
Names:						
	0 1 2	0 1 2	0 1 2	0 1 2	0 1 2	0 1 2
MATTER – 8 marks 1. The arguments used would appeal to the average, reasonable person. 2. A thorough understanding of the topic was displayed. 3. Arguments were well developed and supported with appropriate examples. 4. First speakers: (Topic was clearly defined) Other speakers: (Opposition's arguments were effectively refuted).						
MANNER – 8 marks 1. Speaker was clearly heard. 2. Good eye contact with audience was maintained (palm cards were unobtrusive). 3. Pace of delivery was effective. 4. Speaker's manner was confident and persuasive.						
METHOD (STRUCTURE) – 4 marks 1. Speech was clearly organised into a beginning, a well-developed middle and an end. 2. Good use was made of time allocation. 3. Showed evidence of the roles of different speakers (bonus mark).						
Individual's Total (20)						
Total Team Points (60)						

Progress maps take various forms. Pupils follow unique patterns of growth in any area of learning. Although these patterns are not age related, generalisations can be drawn from them and milestones can be observed and recorded on a progress map. Continuums of development, outcome statement levels and Bandscales are all examples of progress maps. Most progress maps describe behaviours at various stages and incorporate a combination of descriptions of pupil learning and pupil work samples.

Some progress maps, such as outcome statements, reflect big pictures or global descriptions intended for systemic, summative judgements. Others, such as the *First Steps* developmental continuum, use descriptions that can be useful for diagnostic purposes. Some pupils take a long time to move across large, significant outcome levels and then the teachers might prefer to use finer-grained information to indicate that the incremental steps of progress are being made towards outcome levels.

Direct observation is useful when pupils are actively engaged in performance, production, presentation or process. Observational information can be recorded on informal *running records* or a *retrieval chart* or against a predetermined *check-list of criteria*.

Check-lists make it easy for teachers to identify when pupils are able to demonstrate particular learning outcomes. They can be prepared in advance, and should identify a clear set of criteria, to which the teacher and pupils can refer. The criteria can be jointly negotiated. Each time a targeted skill is observed, the appropriate criteria is marked. Space should be allocated for writing informal comments alongside pupil's names. It is important to be unobtrusive while observing pupils and/or small groups as they work, and to allow time between observations to make notes and synthesise the information. The check-lists should be kept, as they are a valuable resource for informing learning programmes, when talking to parents, and when writing reports on individual pupils.

The following check-lists provide an opportunity to note pupils' learning skills, as well as their skills and understanding in a particular learning area.

Problem areas need to be blitzed. Strategies such as explicit teaching, coaching and modelling, and explicit feedback, produce good results. As pupils work on their skills, it is important to continue to observe their progress over a period of time and in a range of contexts. It can be helpful to use a *set of criteria*, a *check-list*, or *retrieval chart* while making observational notes, as a reminder of the focus. This process is called monitoring. It is an ongoing process, and means keeping a close watch on what is to be learned.

LITERACY DEVELOPMENTAL CONTINUUM

Attainment Target 3: Writing

■ Level 1

Pupils' writing communicates meaning through simple words and phrases. In their reading or their writing, pupils begin to show awareness of how full stops are used. Letters are usually clearly shaped and correctly orientated.

■ Level 2

Pupils' writing communicates meaning in both narrative and non-narrative forms, using appropriate and interesting vocabulary, and showing some awareness of the reader. Ideas are developed in a sequence of sentences, sometimes demarcated by capital letters and full stops. Simple, monosyllabic words are usually spelt correctly, and where there are inaccuracies the alternative is phonetically plausible. In handwriting, letters are accurately formed and consistent in size.

■ Level 3

Pupils' writing is often organised, imaginative and clear. The main features of different forms of writing are used appropriately, beginning to be adapted to different readers. Sequences of sentences extend ideas logically and words are chosen for variety and interest. The basic grammatical structure of sentences is usually correct. Punctuation to mark sentences – full stops, capital letters and question marks – is used accurately. Handwriting is joined and legible.

■ Level 4

Pupils' writing in a range of forms is lively and thoughtful. Ideas are often sustained and developed in interesting ways and organised appropriately for the purpose and the reader. Vocabulary choices are often adventurous and words are used for effect. Pupils are beginning to use grammatically complex sentences extending meaning. Spelling, including that of polysyllabic words that conform to regular patterns, is generally accurate. Full stops, capital letters and question marks are used correctly, and pupils are beginning to use punctuation within the sentence. Handwriting style is fluent, joined and legible.

■ Level 5

Pupils' writing is varied and interesting, conveying meaning clearly in a range of forms for different readers, using a more formal style where appropriate. Vocabulary choices are imaginative and words are used precisely. Simple and complex sentences are organised into paragraphs. Words with complex regular patterns are usually spelt correctly. A range of punctuation, including commas, apostrophes and inverted commas, is usually used accurately. Handwriting is joined, clear and fluent and, where appropriate, is adapted to a range of tasks.

■ Level 6

Pupils' writing often engages and sustains the reader's interest, showing some adaptation of style and register to different forms, including using an impersonal style where appropriate. Pupils use a range of sentence structures and varied vocabulary to create effects. Spelling is generally accurate, including that of irregular words. Handwriting, and where appropriate, punctuation is usually used correctly to clarify meaning, and neat and legible. A range of punctuation is usually correctly used. Words are organised into paragraphs.

TRANSITIONAL

Transitional readers and writers are beginning to integrate reading and writing strategies. They read and write a range of text forms, but their writing may be characterised by rigid adherence to known forms. Their writing is becoming more conventional. They are beginning to monitor their comprehension, and their reading strategies appropriately. They are beginning to use visual and meaning-based strategies for word identification and spelling.

TEXT LEVEL – Reading

1 ◆ Is able to discuss purpose for reading
  ◆ Is becoming efficient in using most of following strategies when reading: ma substantiates predictions; self-corrects to confirm meaning; uses visual cu sub-vocalises when encountering diff substitutes familiar words for unknow uses knowledge of print conventions

2 ◆ Can re-tell and discuss own interpre range of texts with familiar concept showing marked preference f information relating to plot and characterisation in fiction or to ma supporting detail in non-fiction tex

◆ Is aware of failure to comprehend use a range of monitoring and adj strategies

3 ◆ Recognises that characters can be a text and can discuss how this co

4 ◆ Selects appropriate material from adjusts reading strategies for dif different purposes eg skims to go and scans for a key word

5 ◆ Is self motivated to read for a r

TEXT LEVEL – Writing

◆ Attempts to orient the reader
◆ Attempts simple planning, e framework or procedure

◆ Writes a range of text forms reports, procedures and exp appropriate purposes, but d these forms

SENTENCE LEVEL – Reading

◆ Is becoming aware of the signalled by a range of co eg therefore, however

◆ Begins to use knowledge punctuation marks to en introduction to compreh is beginning to write text eg understands and uses conjunctions and somet subordinate phrases and 'punctuates simple sent when directed uses pr

◆ EVEL – Reading
  ◆ Is in increasing co luding some diffic ds, eg science, sp eter latitude

◆ ENTENCE LEVEL – Reading
  ◆ eaning efficient tification strate non letter patt articulation wit

◆ EL – Writi
  ◆ ning to u
  m
  ◆ ts all vo
  placing
  ting to ---
  le of common letter p
  ◆ features of words

10 ◆ Is aware of the importance and quality of
  ◆ handwriting
  ◆ Controls basic formations and joins
  ◆ is aware that quality of handwriting is not maintained when focus is on other factors
  deteriorate when
  ◆ new demands of writing

CONVENTIONAL

Reading

Students read a wide range of texts with purpose, understanding and critical awareness.

The student:

R ◆ Responds to texts by demonstrating attending behaviours, recognising common elements and using strategies to
F   access content in printed texts

R ◆ Engages in reading-like behaviour and demonstrates understanding that written symbols and illustrations convey
1   information

R ◆ Uses basic strategies to locate, select and read a range of simple texts; recalls and discusses significant ideas from
2   texts; and understands that people write about real and imagined experiences.

R ◆ Integrates a range of strategies to interpret and discuss relationships between ideas, information and events in
3   written texts; identifies and uses language structures; and recognises the use of symbols and
    descriptions to make meaning

R ◆ Understands how language structures work to shape meaning; explains possible reasons for varying interpretations;
4   and justifies own interpretation of ideas, information and events in texts

R ◆ Discusses and compares texts to construct reasoned responses, ideas and effects; pays attention to synthesising information from
5   different sources to examine issues, ideas and effects; pays attention to synthesising information from
    and purposes

R ◆ Draws on a repertoire of strategies, including knowledge of sociocultural contexts, to maintain understanding while
6   reading, comparing and evaluating different texts containing complex issues

R ◆ Reads critically and discusses a wide range of complex texts; selects substantial evidence to justify own
7   interpretations of those texts and identifies ways in which text structure can influence a reader's reactions

R ◆ Reads critically and reflects on all kinds of texts; lucidly conveys ideas about texts in a compelling way; and relates
8   specific issues and ideas in texts to wider social issues and to personal experience

  ◆ Is aware of a
    accounting to audience una
  ◆ Experiments with artistic or unusual styl
    computer-generated graphics

SMALL GROUP OBSERVATION IN SCIENCE

TOPIC: _____ CLASS: _____

YEAR: _____ DATE: _____

TASK: **Vocabulary in Context**

Pupils' Names						
The pupils were able to:	**Yes/No**	**Yes/No**	**Yes/No**	**Yes/No**	**Yes/No**	**Yes/No**
1. Scan the text effectively	Y/N	Y/N	Y/N	Y/N	Y/N	Y/N
2. Read around the words in order to find clues for their meaning	Y/N	Y/N	Y/N	Y/N	Y/N	Y/N
3. Identify and transfer clues to the *Vocabulary in Context* sheet	Y/N	Y/N	Y/N	Y/N	Y/N	Y/N
4. Transfer the meaning into their own words	Y/N	Y/N	Y/N	Y/N	Y/N	Y/N
5. Justify their interpretation of the meaning	Y/N	Y/N	Y/N	Y/N	Y/N	Y/N

Check-list for the Observation of Small Group Work

Names of Group Members	Group Processes			Subject Understandings – ENERGY AND CHANGE		
	Asks for further clarification or information	Explains individual feelings/ideas	Interrupts/argues politely	Knows how energy is transferred in an energy interaction	Can explain how factors affecting friction can influence design	Can explain at a particle level interactions of energy in energy transfer systems
	Yes/No	Yes/No	Yes/No	Yes/No	Yes/No	Yes/No
Matt	✓✓	✓✓✓	✓✓✓✓ talks too much when others are speaking	✓✓✓		✓✓
Sarah	✓	✓	✓✓	✓✓	✓	✓✓
Phuong	✓	✓✓✓	✓	✓✓	✓	✓✓
John	✓	✓✓✓	✓✓	✓✓	✓	✓✓

Adapted from Clarke, Wideman and Eadie (1990).

Involving the learner – Adolescents are conceptually more sophisticated and are moving towards becoming mature learners. If they are given opportunities jointly to negotiate clear criteria in advance and know what they are supposed to be learning, they don't have to guess what is in the teacher's head. Pupils can be encouraged to take ownership and control over their learning through self and peer assessment activities. Useful tools that involve the learner include *self-evaluation sheets*, reflective *journal writing*, *portfolio assessment* and *peer assessment*.

Discriminating tools that provide diagnostic information – Often the things missing are the techniques and tools to assist with 'kid watching'. A range is provided on the next page.

Central to the task of improving assessment is the collection of baseline data, through the use of potent assessment tools (both qualitative and quantitative) that provide a rich source of diagnostic information. These can be used for a variety of purposes. Data collected at the school level provides a *yardstick* picture of the range of ability across the school. Data collected in the classroom provides a *dipstick* picture of what is happening in every classroom and in every subject area. The analysis of data identifies strengths and weaknesses and indicates where strategies need to be put in place to ensure improvement. As problem areas are targeted, further data collections will indicate whether or not the strategies are working. Ongoing assessment and monitoring processes enable teachers to continue to gather and compare information about the level of pupils' understandings and about their learning skills, and provide accurate information for evaluation purposes.

1. **Pupil evaluation** – a valid and valuable source of information about pupils' perspectives on a task or process, what they understand and what confuses them. May take the form of a check-list, oral reflection, reflective journal writing, conference log recording a pupil/teacher interview.	e.g. 'I can't understand this book; it's too hard …' 'I know how to write topic sentences but I still don't know how to develop and support my ideas.'
2. **Peer evaluation** – pupils can be trained to evaluate their peers effectively against specific criteria.	e.g. 'The ideas in your essay are clearly organised but your essay ends too suddenly.'
3. **Teacher jottings** – about pupil learning behaviour and understandings.	e.g. 'Trevor seems to have difficulty answering inferential questions.'

4. **'On balance' judgements** – a weighing up of pupils' products and processes (completed over time and in a variety of contexts). Pupils' outcomes are measured against a continuum or sequence of outcomes.

A sequence of pupil levels	Level One	Level Two	Level Three	Level Four	Level Five
	___	___	___	___	___
	___	___	___	___	___
	___	___	___	___	___
	___	___	___	___	___

5. **Criteria check-lists** – a planned observation or record of achievement of specific criteria. The teacher records observed pupil outcomes.

Criteria to be observed:	Sam	Joe	Tom	Bev
1.	✓	✓	✗	✓
2.	✓	✓	✗	✓
3.	✗	✓	✗	✓
4.	✓	✓	✓	✓

6. **Anecdotal information** – incidental information that the teacher mentally notes, for example, noting the quality of the questions that pupils ask. Contributes to a balanced picture of achievement.	e.g. 'Vivian takes an awfully long time to find what she's looking for in the library. I must ask her what strategies she uses for accessing information.'
7. **Parent input** – information that is observed in settings outside of school.	e.g. 'Joseph had a lot of trouble with that assignment. He said he didn't know where to start.'
8. **Portfolio** – a collection of meaningful pieces of information that shows pupil achievement of processes and products over time. Contains relevant information using all of the above strategies for collecting information. Is referred to occasionally in order to make 'on balance' judgements.	e.g. 'When viewing this term's work samples, self-evaluation sheets, teacher jottings, criteria check-lists, I can see that Chris has significantly developed his skills in organising and developing his ideas.'

Summary

This section described adolescence as a period between childhood and maturity – a time when teenagers live in the nether world of being a delightful child one moment and a mature adult the next. It described the characteristics that make adolescent learners different to other pupils in other phases of learning. It outlined different learning principles and highlighted a specific set of learning emphases that have particular significance for adolescent learners. This group needs to feel good about themselves as learners. They need to work in a safe environment where they can learn from their mistakes. The quality of teachers' expectations and interactions has a huge impact on pupils' self-esteem, the quality of their work and their school achievement.

The chapter also described the importance of *linking to, recruiting, building on* and *extending* pupils' existing knowledge. It emphasised the fact that adolescent learners love to be actively engaged in a purposeful, motivating and relevant curriculum, and that they all need varying degrees of support to make progress with their learning. It was pointed out that if learning experiences are to be varied and challenging, so too must the assessment regime!

4 Adolescent learners and literacy

In the early years and at primary school there is usually an explicit focus on the teaching of literacy, as there is on the teaching of a range of learning processes. In the middle school, content begins to exert more influence. This is not to deny that many teachers in these year levels continue to teach students how to learn, rather than just what to learn. Nevertheless, the sense of a lot of content to get through begins to emerge in the middle school, before dominating at senior levels.

(Lountain and Dumbleton, 1999b)

At the very time when literacy is required as the key for successful learning, it tends to be overlooked, taken for granted, or relegated to a place of lesser importance. Rather than 'assuming knowledge', it is critical that middle and secondary school teachers recognise the diversity of language development of their pupils and the diversity and language requirements in all subject areas.

Literacy for adolescents should not be taken for granted. Yet it is often the case in middle and secondary schools that nearly everything related to literacy learning *is* taken for granted. It is frequently assumed, for example, that all pupils come to high school able to write and read competently and that they share the same passion for subject matter as their teachers. In the secondary context, pupils face greater exposure to informational texts and these texts can have readability levels beyond their capabilities. It is quite common to find pupils in the one class working with a specified textbook, even though it might be unsuitable for a number of them.

Literacy is the key

Schools have always played a crucial role in determining life opportunities and providing access to language and literacy practices that are considered to be important in society. Those people who have the ability to use language appropriately in a range of contexts and for a variety of purposes have access to a greater number of life choices and are less likely to be manipulated by others' use of language.

School literacy means being able to engage effectively in the language practices reinforced and valued in the school context. It means being able to make meaning of school subjects. Language is an integral part of this making and sharing of subject specific meaning. Teachers and learners use language in the social context of the classroom to make and negotiate meaning, and therefore literacy and language underpin all school learning. Pupils demonstrate their learning and their command of a number of subject languages through the literacy skills of listening, speaking, reading, writing, viewing and critical thinking. Literacy is therefore a tool for learning, as well as an indicator of success at school.

National Literacy Strategy requirements

The NLS requirements for Key Stage 3 form an important part of the context for UK schools. They reflect the importance of focusing on literacy learning for adolescents. They require pupils to be taught objectives related to reading and writing systematically, and suggest the need to develop the pace and accuracy of reading. They also suggest the need to develop inferential and summarisation skills. Writing objectives indicate the need for pupils to be able to make appropriate choices for spelling, to be able to spell multi-syllabic words, to construct complex sentences using subordination and a range of connectives, and to plan and edit a wide range of texts with increasing sophistication. In summary, the key messages about literacy at this stage reinforce the importance of:

- continuity with primary school programmes, especially the literacy hour
- a strong emphasis on the explicit and direct teaching of specified skills in reading and writing, at the word, sentence and text level
- targeted action planning to improve literacy problems, with a focus on specific groups (such as boys)
- using appropriate learning and teaching strategies for adolescent learners.

These requirements are both necessary and demanding. They direct attention to the core component of improving learning in middle and secondary schools, which is to provide pupils with tools to access curriculum literacies.

What adolescent learners face in literacy

Immediate demands

Subject specific literacies

Literacy is not 'one thing', evenly spread across different learning areas. It looks different, and takes on different forms in different subjects and classrooms (Kress, 1999). Each learning area has its own curriculum literacies (subject specific terminology, concepts, skills and understandings) and ways of viewing the world that must be understood. There are some similarities in what pupils might do by way of writing, reading, listening and speaking in each subject area, but the results tend to be different, because each subject uses its own language, conventions and structures. A procedure written in a science or physical education lesson, for example, will not look the same as a procedure written in an English lesson. There may be similarities in the form of the writing, but the terminology, tone and content of the procedure will differ. Pupils have to learn to master these differences.

Increasing literacy demands

A 'literacy demand' refers to any task that requires pupils to use literacy skills to demonstrate skills and/or understandings. The literacy demands of each learning area can differ in both subtle and overt ways, and they increase in complexity and difficulty as pupils move through their schooling.

First Year	*Second Year*	*Third Year*
impact	*satellite*	*nuclear fusion*
comet fragments	*sun synchronous*	*neutron star*
accurate	*geosynchronous*	*absolute magnitude*
nebulae	*infrared light*	*photosphere*
black holes	*remote sensing*	*chromosphere*
quasars	*maria*	*plagues*
pulsars	*microgravity*	*prominences*
perigee	*vaporising*	*emission spectrum*
waning	*power*	*solar stills*
solar eclipse	*gravitational force*	*photovoltaic cell*
kuiper belt	*cosmonauts*	*interstellar*
neap tide		*spicules*

(Examples from Heinemann (1996), *Outcomes: Science Books 1–4*)

Those who struggle to meet the literacy demands of different subject areas are likely to have difficulty adequately demonstrating effective learning outcomes. In every lesson, pupils face a wide range of challenging literacy demands. They have to be able to recognise, understand and use the specialised vocabulary of the subject:

peninsula

theme

vaporisation

sparingly soluble

SYMBOL

PASCALS PROGRAMS

metaphor

monarchy

hypothesis

miesosis

friction

e-cosystem   rotational
symmetry   mitosis

RATINGS

RATIO

National Dietary
Guidelines

theology

apparatus

NUTRITION

plate separation   protein-rich

precipitation   measures of
central tendency

principles of
movement

COMMERCIAL

protons

point of view

input, processing
and output   off-side

spreadsheet

Neutral

Agrarian
Revolution

Neutrons

dependent variable

narrator

areas of dissection

proletariat   The   base

balanced
diet

Scientific Method

Third

World   minor
analgesics

dictorial powers

caricature

climate regions

Conclusion

Statute
law   air pressure

large capacity

character   plot

mainframe
computers

They have to be able to read, make meaning of, locate and extract important information embedded in different genres and in subject specific texts:

Inertia also works on moving bodies. A body in motion will keep moving at the same speed and in the same direction (uniform motion) unless some outside force is exerted on it and causes some change. The moving body's inertia is its property of resisting my attempt to change its motion.

PQRST is a square-based pyramid with a base of side length 14mm, and height of 6mm. The point X is vertically below T on the base, and point Y is midway along PQ.

I collapsed in the armchair in a fit of despair. I had no way of knowing if my thoughts and feelings had actually reached her in some way and motivated her phone call, or if she had simply followed some intuition of her own.

The **climates** of Europe are dominated by the **westerlies**. These are **on-shore winds** that blow from the Atlantic Ocean. They are associated with **rain-bearing depressions (low pressure areas)** called **mid-latitude** lows. Mid-latitude lows produce the cool, cloudy and damp weather so common in north-western Europe.

Rare earth metals (lanthanides) are used to make very powerful super magnets. Ferrite used in ordinary magnesdynium (a rare earth) can make a super magnet. In medicine, super magnets are used in extremely sensitive probes that provide scans inside the human body.

They must internalise and then transform information into a variety of written or oral forms that demonstrate their understanding.

The water in a mountain stream is usually crystal clear. After heavy rain, however, the stream would become muddy. Explain, in your own words, why this is so.

Describe what happened to the mothballs. Draw a picture to illustrate your observations.

Make a scale diagram showing the earth's timeline from its beginning up until now, showing the first life, dinosaurs at 200 million years ago, and the first early humans at 2 million years.

What is the difference between speed and velocity?

Footprints left in sand on the earth's surface last a very short time. Why should footprints on the moon last for thousands of years?

Define the word 'drug'. Explain why tobacco and alcohol are drugs.

What are the major uses of uranium? Why is the mining of uranium so controversial?

What other forms of biochemical evidence are there to support evolution?

Multiplicity of tasks

Pupils must also become adept at interpreting digital literacy, at reading and writing multimedia texts, at using different learning technologies, at critically analysing and interpreting new types of texts in different ways, and at understanding how texts explicitly and implicitly influence them.

Recent research (Wyatt-Smith and Cumming, 1999) suggests that teachers can often be unaware of the literacy demands they place on pupils. When pupils reach senior school, the explicit teaching of literacy tends to stop. They are expected to tackle a range of writing, speaking, listening, interpreting and critical thinking demands simultaneously. One pupil, observed in a science classroom during the study, was:

> *... interpreting a stream of rapid verbal English from his teacher, and the writing and layout information on an overhead transparency. He was writing layout diagrams, symbolic notations, and mathematics in his personal notebook; observing the teacher's gestures, blackboard diagrams and writing, observing the actions and speech of other students, including their manipulation of demonstration apparatus, and the running commentary of his next-seat neighbour. In fact, he quite often had to integrate and co-ordinate most of these either simultaneously or within a span of a few minutes. There is no way he could have kept up with the content development and conceptual flow of these lessons without integrating at least a few of these different literacy modes almost constantly.*

(Lemke, 1999, p.23)

These types of demands are compounded for many pupils, because in some subject areas:

> *many of the words are new or unfamiliar, the meanings being made are about strange matters of which he/she has no personal experience, the diagrams and graphs and formulas may bear only an outline resemblance to any seen before, the problems are difficult for his/her current level of mastery, the subject matter is abstract, and the problems of mutual co-ordination and calibration of all of these channels and literacies and activities are very substantial indeed.*

(Lemke, 1999, p.23)

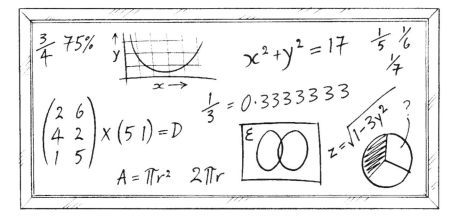

Pupils must cope with these literacy tasks, not just in one classroom, but in a range of classrooms, every hour, every day, and every week.

The changing nature of literacy

Literacy is not static. It can look different in the workplace, in the home and across schools, because different cultures and contexts require, reinforce and promote literacies that are valued in that community. Pupils at inner city schools and pupils in rural schools, for example, will participate in very different practices.

From a single literacy to multiliteracies

Our understandings about what it means to be literate change as society changes. In the past, it was possible to participate effectively in society using only *functional* literacy skills (such as correct paragraphing, spelling, sentence structure and grammar). These skills are still vitally important today, but effective participation in society now also requires knowledge of how to understand and apply a range of literacies, including *digital, critical, technological, visual, cultural* and *multiliteracies.*

New technologies are rapidly changing our understandings about literacy and the way we use language. Adolescent learners are becoming more proficient at handling, locating, analysing, extracting, storing and using increasing amounts of information. They are having to understand and apply a much wider range of literacy skills than their earlier counterparts, for a wider variety of purposes. As new methods of communication emerge, they will continue to develop new ways of accessing, using and combining information into different types of texts.

In the future, adolescents will have to learn to become readers, writers and users of new computer-based media and multimedia genres that combine visuals, sound and words in non-linear patterns with graphics, images and video. They will be required to think, design text and solve problems in new ways, as they 'use, browse and co-author the text' (Snyder, 1996, p.73). Pupils are already familiar with the Web and e-mail, digital cameras, CD Roms, laptop computers and multimedia texts and they are able to 'surf across television channels; amble along electronic mailboxes; browse through the Internet, or 'club' around with bulletin board pals' (Luke, 1995, p.17).

The New London Group (1996) suggests that a multiplicity of literacies (or multiliteracies) will be used in the future. This term incorporates cultural, as well as visual, audio, spatial, behavioural and multimodal methods of communication that will result from rapid technological advances, at a global level.

> *As we create new ways of communicating with one another, we develop new genres of written language that need to be read in new ways. We gain the possibility of combining the written word with graphic animation, sound and video in new multimedia genres. The lives of this generation and the next will be profoundly changed by these new computer-based media, genres or texts.*
>
> (Lemke, 1995)

Technology is moving forwards at a rapid rate, and has already had a profound impact on the way teachers and schools operate. In some classrooms, there is a widening gulf between the teacher's and pupils' experiences with technology. Some teachers feel threatened by the fact that they do not have the same expertise as their pupils, and claim that they are faced with 'aliens in the classroom'. As learning technologies become commonplace, it is likely that teachers without some degree of expertise will feel like the 'aliens in the classroom' (Bigum and Green, 1993a).

As with any tool for learning, pupils have to have exposure to, and opportunities to practise using different technologies. They need to be able to decide whether or not the technology will *help them to achieve their purpose*, and whether or not it will be *available* at the time when it is needed. A key factor for learning is being able to select the most appropriate technology to fulfil a particular task.

New demands will be placed on teachers in the future, who will need to develop and teach the skills needed to master these new technologies. Pupils will demonstrate a range of competencies, and some might already be experienced users of new genres. The notion of a *community of learners* will become more important in the future because pupils and teachers will need to share and pool their expertise and knowledge.

From functional to critical literacy

It is imperative that pupils gain mastery over language. They must be able to communicate effectively with others, using universally accepted conventions. Functional literacy is therefore not an option. It is non-negotiable. However, as adolescents move towards adulthood, they will need much more than the basic learning tools to enable them to make progress outside school. Today's curriculum has to work, not only in the present, but for the future (Kress, 1999) and therefore teachers and schools cannot concentrate solely on functional literacy. They cannot ignore computer, visual, critical, cultural and all the other multiliteracies that pupils are already starting to face now and will increasingly face in the future.

As pupils engage with these new forms of literacy, they will need to be equipped with skills that they can use to analyse the validity and source of information. Critical literacy approaches recognise that meaning is not fixed in, or by, texts, and that it is possible to have multiple, optional and contradicting interpretations of the one text. They also recognise that texts, as 'versions of reality', carry values of power, gender and race, and that they shape the way in which pupils construct their world.

Much of the information that adolescents access from texts, the Internet and television is unmediated. It is becoming increasingly important that pupils know how texts work, how they situate and manipulate readers and how they position them to read or interpret situations in particular ways. Without the tools to carry out this type of critical analysis, they are left vulnerable to manipulation.

There is a fine line, then, in balancing the need to teach the fundamental basics of language (functional literacy), with the need to attend to the other literacies that also need to be mastered. All of these literacies are important, because they reflect the reality of the world today, as well as the world of tomorrow.

The hectic and rapid changes occurring in society today are not going to disappear, and therefore our understandings about literacy will need to continue to evolve as society changes. It is difficult to predict the kinds of literacies that will be valued in the future, but there is no doubt that language and literacy will continue to be a key requirement for successful participation in future society. Those who are unable to master the use of language will be virtually disempowered. Getting the balance right between functional literacy and multiliteracies is therefore important. And getting the balance right will continue to be an ongoing challenge for teachers and schools!

Literacy is the linchpin that gives adolescents the confidence to move into Key Stage 4 and then out into the adult world.

Establishing a whole school approach

A *whole school approach* to literacy ensures that the breadth of achievement within the school is recognised, and that consistency and continuity is demonstrated in teaching, learning and assessment practices across all classrooms.

A whole school *literacy policy* enables all teachers to come to common understandings about literacy, and to articulate a set of values about literacy that all teachers support.

Whole School Policy on literacy

All teachers at _____ school are teachers of literacy.

Current understandings about literacy include the knowledge that it is not possible to teach the communication (literacy) skills of listening, speaking, reading, viewing and writing in one or two forty minute English lessons each week and to expect that these skills will then spill over into every learning area.

Nor are the literacy demands of each learning area the same. Each has its own subject specific vocabulary, content, concepts, understandings and skills which have to be understood, reinforced, practised and developed so that students can internalise them. Each learning area emphasises different ways of using language – a procedure written for an English lesson, for example will not look the same as one written for a Science lesson. The form of writing may bear similarities, but the terminology, tone and content will differ. Literacy skills therefore need to be explicitly taught and reinforced by <u>every teacher in every learning area of the curriculum</u> and students need to be provided with many opportunities to practise, develop and refine their literacy skills.

In each classroom we have students who demonstrate a wide spread of ability levels. BCC promotes development learning principles and therefore students' different learning styles and different rates of learning should be catered for. In order to accommodate this diverse range it is important that teachers have knowledge of a wide range of strategies from which they are able to select those which best cater for students' needs, abilities and interests.

The *Stepping Out* program is presented each year. The aim of the program is to build on teachers' skills in order to improve students' learning outcomes. Our whole school approach to literacy ensures that we recognise the breadth of achievement within our school and that we demonstrate consistency and continuity in terms of our teaching and assessment practices.

Kiddey (1995)

The literacy leader and/or members of the literacy committee have an important role to play in a whole school approach. They have the expertise to discuss, explain and model ways in which particular literacy strategies can be incorporated within subject specific content, as well as strategies that will effectively target the whole school literacy priority. This can be done at the classroom, learning area or whole school level. When teachers share common understandings about pupils' needs and about the effectiveness of particular literacy and learning strategies, they are able to work to effect improvement.

As part of the literacy policy, many schools implement a whole school *literacy audit.* They seek out data where gaps in information are detected. They might decide to conduct a whole school testing programme, to provide baseline information about pupils' skills. Teachers collect, collate and analyse qualitative/quantitative data about pupils' literacy levels from all learning areas and various sources across the school.

Learning Team Literacy Overview

Year	Teacher/ No. of Students		Low Scores			High Scores		
			Reading	Writing		Reading	Writing	
			Torch Stanine 3 ↓	TAWE – Less Than 15/30	Total	TORCH Stanine8/9	TAWE 27 - 30	Total
A TEAM								
7	A1	31	1	5		20	0	
7	A2	31	1	6		18	3	
7	A 3	31	5	7		8	1	
8	A 4	27	5	2		7	7	
8	A 5	30	3	2		15	5	
8	A 6	29	1	4		12	0	
		179	**16**	**26**	**42**	**80**	**16**	**96**
B TEAM								
8	B 1	31	-	2		8	1	
8	B 2	28	1	4		7	0	
7	B 3	27	2	12		10	1	
7	B 4	31	2	5		14	0	
8	B 5	29	2	4		18	2	
8	B 6	22	2	4		8	1	
		168	**9**	**31**	**40**	**65**	**5**	**70**
C TEAM								
8	C 1	30	2	2		13	3	
8	C 2	30	4	2		8	1	
7	C 3	30	7	5		11	2	
7	C 4	30	6	6		7	0	
7	C 5	30	2	8		15	1	
ESU	C 6	8	5	8		0	0	
		158	**26**	**31**	**57**	**54**	**7**	**61**
D TEAM								
8	D 1	29	3	5		9	1	
8	D 2	28	1	10		11	1	
7	D 3	32	7	11		7	2	
7	D 4	31	6	10		7	0	
7	D 5	29	6	9		9	2	
STAR	D 6	9	5	9		0	0	
		158	**28**	**54**	**82**	**43**	**6**	**49**
E TEAM								
9	E 1	29	3	0		10	6	
9	E 2	28	4	2		11	9	
9	E 3	32	2	1		16	18	
9	E 4	31	8	2		8	10	
9	E 5	29	3	1		13	9	
		147	**20**	**6**	**26**	**58**	**52**	**110**
F TEAM								
9	F 1	31	3	1		7	4	
9	F 2	31	4	0		11	3	
9	F 3	31	3	3		3	4	
9	F 4	30	2	5		10	4	
		123	**12**	**9**	**21**	**31**	**15**	**46**

Overview of learning team literacy levels (Kiddey 1995)

Debates about issues related to the use of teacher judgements or test results can be avoided if the best aspects of both approaches are implemented. Teacher judgements, based on detailed knowledge of the students, over time and over a variety of situations, clearly have more validity than a one off test which is probably only partially relevant. But these take time, can be hard to collate, and may lack a common standard.

The ongoing collection and analysis of data highlights areas that need to be addressed. Teachers can be informed of the findings of the whole school audit and can vote for a *whole literacy priority focus*, that will be addressed by all teachers, in all learning areas.

A whole school literacy focus

There are many advantages in having a whole school or subject area literacy focus that all teachers agree to teach, monitor and report on.

Once a literacy priority has been determined, learning areas need collaboratively to develop an action plan that targets the area of need. The plan would need to identify the amount of support that team members might need to tackle the literacy priority. They would also need to consider target outcomes, related strategies, ways to collect and collate data, resource/role allocations, timelines and a set of criteria for determining success.

Literacy teachers and/or members of the Literacy Management Team are well placed to be able collaboratively to develop a set of criteria that can be used as a monitoring tool for the literacy priority, and to co-ordinate the collection and analysis of data. The ongoing assessment and monitoring of data indicates whether or not the combined efforts of all teachers is making a difference!

The literacy focus can be reviewed at regular intervals and changed according to need. In this way, the school (or subject area) continually works towards improving pupils' learning outcomes.

Whole School Literacy Focus

Students will develop active and attentive listening skills

Today you will receive (personally or through your *Literacy and Learning Committee* member) the data collection proforma for monitoring listening skills in your classroom.

The proforma has been divided into the three categories which teachers identified earlier in the term as being of concern:

- *listening for instructions*
- *listening for manners (individually, in small groups, and in the classroom)*
- *listening for main ideas (supporting details, translating information etc.)*

The process is simple.

Please select two students (one lower ability/one average ability) from your class. (Student 1 = lower ability. Student 2 = average ability.)

The proforma is double sided (one page per student). Write the number (i.e. 1 or 2 – *see the code above*) and the student's name in the space allocated at the top of one of the two pages, and complete the other relevant details in the top section of the page.

Reflect on any checklists/anecdotal information of listening behaviour (etc.) that you have collected over the past weeks; in-class observations you have made; levels you might have previously placed them on; and then read the outcome pointers on the proforma.

After reflection, please use your professional judgement to tick off the appropriate pointers achieved by the student for each category.

Your completed proforma can then be handed to your Team Literacy and Learning Committee member, who will photocopy all team proformas. Originals will be returned. Committee members will collate, analyse, record and report back the whole school picture at a team meeting. We hope to be able to collect all proformas by Monday/Tuesday afternoon. We are grateful for your co-operation...

Example of the monitoring process (Kiddey, 1995)

(Teachers used a simple framework to record levels of achievement. These were collated and reported back at the whole school level.)

Determining where the school is at with regards to literacy understandings

Sometimes it is useful to collect baseline data about understandings of literacy – within a subject area, or at the school level. The following *Stepping Out* (1995) framework, which was featured in the 1999 LEA Key Stage 3 file, can be used to identify strategies that need to be put in place to move teachers (and the school) forward. It can be used, or reviewed at different times, to identify whether strategies put in place have been effective.

Where are we now? Links between literacy and learning

LEVEL	EMERGING	DEVELOPING	FUNCTIONAL	EMBEDDED
Level of Whole School Commitment	• English teachers and literacy/learning support teachers accept their role as teachers of literacy. • Some teachers share literacy and learning related information about materials and strategies used. • There is no recognition of the need for a cross-curricular approach to literacy and learning improvement.	• The school has identified a need to address the students' literacy and learning needs and individual subject departments have independently introduced strategies to address literacy improvement. • The school is experiencing difficulties in developing a whole school approach and commitment to literacy and learning improvement.	• There is a whole school priority in literacy. Attempts have been made to establish cross-curriculum communication structures in order to develop a unified view of and commitment to literacy and learning improvement. • Strong leadership exists in some areas of the school.	• All teachers in all subject departments accept their role as teachers of literacy in the context of teaching subject content. • The school has a long term view of literacy and learning improvement and commits time each year for whole school planning to address achievable short term goals for literacy and learning improvement. • There is strong leadership at all levels and a high degree of staff collaboration across the curriculum.
Staff Professional Development	• A few teachers have been provided with quality professional development in literacy and learning. • Staff have not seen the need to participate in professional development in this area.	• Some time has been allocated to providing staff with information on literacy and learning. • The professional development may not be linked to classroom practice.	• Many teachers in many subject departments have undergone quality, professional development in literacy and learning. • The P.D. results in some teachers changing their teaching behaviours. • New staff are inducted into condensed professional development in literacy and learning.	• A significant majority of teachers in all subject departments have undergone quality professional development in literacy. The quality professional development was characterised by: * the availability of theory, demonstration, practice, feedback and coaching; * a climate of peer support; * spaced learning; * a whole school approach; * action research. • The professional development resulted in teacher reflection and the embedding of literacy strategies in the teaching of content. • Each year new staff undergo on-going quality professional development in literacy learning.

LEVEL	EMERGING	DEVELOPING	FUNCTIONAL	EMBEDDED
Delivery of Learning/ Teaching Processes	• The emphasis on the curriculum is content and the delivery of content is pitched 'at the middle' of the class. • Students with identified literacy and learning needs are placed in English focus classes.	• There is a recognition that literacy skills impact on student outcomes however curriculum and school structures impede desires to address this perceived need. • Some teachers are varying the delivery and modifying the content of courses to address whole classes' literacy and learning needs.	• The administration team and some subject departments are supporting change in curriculum and school structures in order to develop students' literacy and learning processes and skills. • Teachers are aware of the need to assess the literacy demands of texts and tasks set.	• The assessment of the literacy demands of texts and tasks set is embedded in the practice of teachers. • All subject departments vary the delivery and adapt the content of courses to address individual students' literacy and learning needs. • School policies acknowledge research that supports intervention in the mainstream.
Monitoring and Evaluating	• The monitoring and evaluation of literacy is perceived as the domain of the English Department. • Students in year eight are assessed during the year in order to stream. • Information from the primary schools is not used to inform the secondary school. • A few individual teachers monitor students' literacy improvement in the context of teaching subject content in order to inform teaching and learning experiences.	• The collation of data is limited to the use of standardised tests. The information collected is used to place students in appropriate units in English.	• There is a recognition that the monitoring and evaluation of literacy is the responsibility of all teachers. • Whole school monitoring of literacy and learning has been set in place. • Teachers are developing the skills to monitor students at the classroom level.	• The school has set in place the collection of high quality longitudinal data to measure whole school literacy and learning improvement. • Teacher judgements are valued in the assessing and monitoring of student performance. • Most teachers are well equipped to monitor individual students' literacy improvement in the context of teaching subject content to inform teaching and learning experiences.
Students' Literacy Outcomes	• Very few students are well equipped to handle the literacy and learning demands of all subject areas.	• The students' literacy and learning skills cover a wide range and there is a significant proportion of students who require high levels of teacher support.	• Whilst many students are adequately equipped to handle the literacy and learning demands of subject areas, it is the teachers' judgement that many students are not achieving their potential.	• Most students have a repertoire of literacy and learning strategies which they independently apply across the curriculum.

Stepping Out (1995). As featured in the LEA NLS Key Stage 3 file (1999).

Designing support at the school level

Mastering school literacies means mastering curriculum literacies. In each subject, literacy involves learning to use its specialised language, its distinctive vocabulary, as well as its symbolic, graphic, pictorial and diagrammatic respresentations. Teachers and learners use language to make and negotiate meaning of subject specific content in the social context of the classroom. Together they use language to read, write and talk about subject specific content. What students read and write about, what they say, and how they say it, is unique to the particular context of the learning area. Literacy is therefore not something added on, or treated separately within a learning area. It is the vehicle for communicating and understanding subject specific content (Chapman, 1996, p4).

Attending to literacy and mastering subject content are therefore two sides of the same coin. Pupils need support to be able to understand and effectively use the specific language of different learning areas. When pupils' literacy skills are improved they process information more effectively, they have greater understandings about subject specific content, and their learning outcomes are improved.

All pupils need support to help them to make progress with their learning. Some will manage with a modicum of assistance, but others will need more targeted support. Maintaining consistent, quality support can be difficult in the middle and secondary school context, because of frequent changes of teachers and subjects.

Whilst it is not practical to attempt to provide a different learning programme for every pupil in every class, it is not beneficial simply to 'teach to the middle of the class' and hope for the best. The needs of adolescent learners can best be met through combinations of whole class teaching, small group work and individual tuition. The teacher must plan how to use these different combinations of groupings, and must also move from group to group, or individual to individual, teaching at the point of need. It has to be said that juggling all of these needs and differences is not an easy task!

The majority of schools provide support at a variety of levels.

Support through withdrawal of pupils

Some schools use withdrawal classes. Pupils at educational risk are withdrawn from class to work (individually, or within a small group) with a support teacher. Withdrawal groups are not often favoured in secondary schools unless they are conducted for short periods of time, for specific purposes, and learning progress is monitored. There is a danger that gaps in learning will widen when withdrawal activities are unrelated to the regular curriculum, and therefore the reason for withdrawal (i.e. to improve learning outcomes) can be defeated.

Let me get this straight – we're behind the rest of the class and we're going to catch up to them by going slower than they are?

(Bart Simpson, 1996)

Research tends not to recommend withdrawal models, because of the 'modelling' benefits that occur in the mainstream classroom and because of the negative labelling attached to withdrawal. Common sense, however, needs to be applied to each situation. Little is gained if these learners remain in the mainstream classroom and their needs are ignored. Nor is anything gained if they consistently receive little or no explicit literacy instruction across classes. Some pupils will, no doubt, pick up literacy skills through osmosis – or learn them 'on the job'. The majority, however, will continue to fall through the net.

The aim of any intervention programme is to improve learning outcomes. Withdrawal activities are not all ineffective. Gifted and talented pupils are often withdrawn so that they can work with pupils of similar abilities and interests. Pupils at educational risk also benefit from participating in special projects that enhance their self-esteem. There is no joy in continually failing in the mainstream classroom.

Programmes that enable pupils at educational risk to engage in carefully planned, rewarding language experience activities can be extremely beneficial. They need, however, to be short, motivational and targeted. Specific outcomes and a set of criteria should be determined in advance and data needs to be collected at regular intervals, so that progress can be closely monitored.

The literacy support/team teacher model

In some schools, pupils remain in their regular classes and move from teacher to teacher. A literacy support teacher might occasionally support the mainstream teacher. Variations of team teaching can occur. The support teacher might take a whole class, small group or individual through aspects of literacy while the regular teacher focuses on the content. Alternatively, the support teacher might take the class while the regular teacher moves around, teaching at the point of need. They plan the learning programme together.

Generally, little explicit teaching of literacy occurs once the support has been removed, because mainstream teachers may not have the knowledge and training to support pupils who are encountering difficulty. This means that these pupils' at-risk status is likely to increase. A worse case scenario happens when the at-risk pupil moves across classrooms – with no teacher having the skills to cater for his or her learning needs. Too often, mainstream teachers remain disempowered because they lack the skills or confidence to know what to do.

The English department support model

The majority of secondary school support models promote a model of literacy support where one or two literacy teachers, or members of the English department, take on the responsibility of monitoring literacy across the school. Whilst these roles are vitally important, it is difficult for one or two people (or several members of one learning area) to be stretched adequately across the school so that all pupils or teachers needing assistance get the help they need.

Skills learned in one 40 or 50-minute English period are not always transferred to other subject areas, because each subject area uses language differently, and for different purposes. A focus in one area of the curriculum does not necessarily support the successful and independent application of literacy skills across all subjects. When schools rely exclusively on the literacy support teacher or English department model, mainstream classroom teachers get a very clear message that literacy is something that 'others' do, that it is hard, that only 'experts' can take it on board, that it is not their responsibility to teach literacy, and that literacy is something that can be 'fixed' in 50 minutes. They become dependent on other people to improve their pupils' literacy skills. Many believe that if the literacy support teacher is working with their pupils, then their pupils' literacy problems are being adequately catered for, and little else needs to be done.

The sharing of responsibility model

Literacy skills need to be consistently worked at. Spasmodic campaigns for literacy improvement tend to be ineffective in the long term. What is needed is a sustained and consistent approach to literacy. Many schools have found that sharing responsibility for literacy amongst teachers (at the subject area, year group, or whole school level) makes the task of literacy improvement much easier. Whilst the work completed in each subject area might be different, common aspects about literacy (*spelling/grammar, paragraphing writing, written and oral genres, note-making skills and research processes*) can be explicitly taught, reinforced and monitored by teachers in a range of subject areas. When teachers work towards common goals for literacy improvement, pupils' literacy skills tend to improve in all subject areas.

Whole school models for literacy improvement have many benefits. Firstly, energy is harnessed towards the one direction and funding can be put aside for resources linked to improvement. Pupils get plenty of opportunities to practise, develop, refine and consolidate their literacy skills – in the context of different subject area content, by the teachers who know the language of their subject better than anyone else. This does not necessarily mean that all teachers need to become literacy teachers, rather than subject area teachers. It does mean, though, that they need to become familiar with a wide range of strategies that can be used to help them to support pupils as they tackle the literacy demands of the subject area.

The volunteer or peer tutor model

Some schools find volunteer or peer tutor programmes to be a beneficial and supportive component of their school literacy improvement strategy. Pupils' self-esteem is markedly raised because of the nurturing nature of the support and encouragement that they receive during the programme. The aim of the programme is negated if volunteer and pupil do not get on well, so care needs to be taken to ensure that close matching occurs. All stakeholders benefit when a training programme is provided by key teachers at the school. Volunteers or peer tutors need to be provided with a range of short activities that reinforce subject specific content or target specific literacy skills. They also need to have a regular forum where they can discuss issues, share ideas and receive support.

Focusing on literacy at the classroom level

Some things can be done in the short term to implement a strategy for improving literacy. The following section outlines the importance of the following:

– Awareness
– Planning
– Action
– Reflection.

Awareness

The most crucial thing that teachers can do is to be aware of what adolescent learners face in the middle and secondary school context. This means observing pupils closely as they go about their work and noting where the problem areas lie. It might mean selecting an aspect of literacy (listening, speaking, writing, reading or critical thinking) and looking closely for literacy demands embedded in related oral, writing and reading activities, tasks, texts and practices.

A teacher's day is often so busy that 'stopping to look' is not something that is built into the planning. It can be interesting to make time to observe what is actually happening – to look closer, for example, at the quantity and quality of talk that takes place. Who does all the talking? What is talked about? What opportunities do pupils get to talk things through? Is interactive small group work encouraged? In writing – what happens to spelling errors in pupils' work? Are they circled by the teacher, and then largely ignored by pupils? Do pupils ever get time to go back over two or three assignments, note feedback and set goals for improvement? Sometimes pupils don't realise that they repeat the same spelling errors frequently, or that several teachers from different subjects have written similar feedback about their work.

It may be useful to reflect on whether pupils get opportunities to read a portion of text silently before being asked to read it orally. If not, they are sight-reading material. Are they expected to remember lengthy instructions, without having key actions listed on the board? Are some tasks too difficult for them to master – would it help if tasks were broken down into smaller, more manageable components?

Without this kind of analysis at the classroom, subject area, year group and/or whole school level, teachers will continue to be oblivious to the literacy demands they place on pupils. Sometimes informal observations don't provide accurate information about an aspect of literacy or learning. It might be necessary to collect baseline data to identify problem areas. This can be done through the use of survey forms, questionnaires, check-lists, retrieval charts or video recordings.

Planning

Once problem areas have been determined (through observation or analysis of data) and targets for improvement have been set, then careful planning needs to take place to ensure that all pupils will be able to reach those targets. Opportunities need to be incorporated for specific literacy skills to be reinforced at various points of the learning journey. It is important to build these moments in, because the explicit teaching of literacy skills takes time and these skills need to be taught and reinforced several times. They are not something that can be taught once, and then left to chance. If the final outcome of a programme of work, for example, involves writing a persuasive argument, time will need to be allocated for teacher and class jointly to negotiate a writing framework for the persuasive argument genre. Time will need to be allocated to discuss the conventions and structure of the genre. Pupils will need ongoing tuition and support, as well as opportunities to practise, develop and refine the skills required to write a powerful persuasive argument.

Literacy demands increase in number and in complexity as pupils move through their schooling. This is another reason why literacy skills need to be explicitly taught in lower secondary school and then continually reinforced each year: the skills then become tools for learning that can be applied independently. When pupils have a range of strategies under their belt, they are able to concentrate on the complex concepts and tasks that have to be tackled in upper school.

Action

Analysis without active response leads nowhere. Once problem areas have been determined and new target outcomes set, strategies need to be put in place to support movement towards the target(s). The selection of support strategies requires careful consideration, because incorrect selection can actually hinder the learning process. Adolescent learners are not grown-up primary school children. They need developmentally appropriate strategies or strategies that have been modified for them. 'One size fits all' approaches such as guided or shared reading (where aspects of the text are highlighted and discussed) need to be used with discrimination and in different ways, because some of these learners are already forming adult relationships and are physically mature. Adolescents like to 'melt' into the crowd, and don't relish undue attention. They are particularly resistant to anything that 'smells' of primary school work, or to work that draws attention to the fact that they might be struggling.

Pupils, as well as teachers, need to build up their own repertoire of strategies that they can 'dip into' for various purposes. This means that they need to be given opportunities to learn about the purpose of different strategies, to practise implementing them, and to reflect on their effectiveness. They will become more adept at selecting appropriate strategies for tasks if they are regularly given opportunities to select from a range.

Performance improves with practice. Tennis players get better at tennis by practising. Saxophonists play more proficiently when they have plenty of practice. It's the same with language. Pupils become more accomplished users of subject specific language when they hear it, see it, speak it, and write it. They have to be exposed to it, to be able to 'approximate' it and to be given opportunities to refine it, before they can apply it confidently. Teachers who model ways of using language in informal talk and class discussions, who highlight and explain key words encountered in texts, and who encourage the use of glossaries and journal writing will find that pupils start to use the language of the subject area naturally, without realising they are doing so.

Adolescent learners need to be able to practise using language in order to get better at using it. They use language to demonstrate their understandings. It is important that time is provided for them to engage in these processes. They need to be able to think things through, to talk and write (in order to clarify ideas), to explore concepts and to explain their thinking. They need to do these things independently as well as in collaboration with others. As they do so, they enrich and extend their vocabulary, as well as their proficiency with language.

Reflection

Without reflection, learning plateaus out or slows down. Reflective thinkers question and assess all aspects of their learning. They identify what they did well, what they might need to do next, and then think about things they might do to improve the learning next time. This type of thinking enables them to be active, independent and self-directed in their approaches to learning tasks. It prevents them from repeating behaviours and ensures that they make progress with their learning.

As they become more proficient at this type of reflection, they develop higher level skills of thinking, or metacognitive skills, and are able to monitor and regulate their own learning. These skills include elements of analysis, problem solving and evaluation. Strategies, such as journal writing or three level questions (which probe for evidence, or require inferences to be made), provide opportunities for pupils to practise using higher level thinking processes.

Teachers also benefit from engaging in reflective practices. They can reflect on the quality and quantity of pupils' learning. They can use reflective thinking processes to inform their practice and to determine the effectiveness of particular strategies on pupils' learning outcomes.

If reflection reveals that pupils are making little or no progress, then it will be necessary to change tactics. This might mean modifying or changing the learning programme. For some pupils, it might mean modifying the learning programme many times until they start to make progress. For others, the repertoire of strategies might need to be extended and built up, and readability of texts might be re-examined. Some skills may need to be explicitly taught, and retaught, so that pupils can focus for a longer period of time on a specific skill.

Summary

This section described the types of literacy demands that adolescent learners face in the middle and secondary school context. It highlighted the fact that different subject areas have their own curriculum literacies (subject specific terminology, concepts, skills and understandings) and their own ways of viewing the world. The changing nature of literacy means that pupils will need to be provided with skills that enable them to tackle functional literacy skills as well as a range of critical, digital, technological, visual, cultural and multiliteracies that they will encounter in the future.

The benefits of whole school approaches to literacy were emphasised. Whole school approaches ensure consistency across all classrooms. They also enable teachers to share the same understandings, and to work towards shared goals. All schools use different strategies to support 'at risk' pupils, and the advantages and disadvantages of many of these strategies were outlined. Particular importance was placed on the need to be aware of the literacy demands of their learning area, on the need to include time for teaching literacy skills when planning lessons, on the importance of actively blitzing problem areas, and on the need to reflect on things that might be put in place to further improve learning.

5 Improving support for teachers

The challenge of improving learning for adolescents is a key issue for schools and school systems. Sustaining improvement is a vexing problem. Many schools achieve success consistently, sometimes in the most trying circumstances. Other schools find that it is difficult to replicate progress elsewhere, and that it is difficult to be sure that pupils who struggled to learn in the past are finally on the road to continued success.

The six reminders

Improving learning for adolescents in middle and secondary schools requires a consistent, well-resourced, long-term effort. There is no easily applied formula or guarantee of an instant solution. The key messages emphasised throughout this text, which seem to form the basis for lasting improvements in learning, can be summarised in a series of six reminders:

- *Reminder 1:* Be aware of the importance of context
- *Reminder 2:* Focus on literacy in subject areas
- *Reminder 3:* Emphasise the appropriate learning principles
- *Reminder 4:* Use practical strategies
- *Reminder 5:* Work on a variety of fronts
- *Reminder 6:* Expand the repertoire

Be aware of the importance of context

There is something special and different about the school context in which adolescents learn. These differences need to be heeded. They need to be understood, analysed and worked with, and those elements that can be changed need to be changed. Effective leadership and a supportive culture are vital ingredients for success.

Focus on literacy in subject areas

Literacy is the key to improving learning in middle and secondary schools. There is a need to move on from generalised notions of language across the curriculum to focus on:

– the literacy demands of each learning area
– responding to these demands specifically, explicitly, consistently and practically
– functional literacy and the literacies required for the new millennium.

Emphasise the appropriate learning principles

Adolescent learners are different. They need to be responded to in ways that reflect those differences. The responses need to be based on learning principles that are:

– grounded in research and well-tested observation
– powerful enough to sustain lasting, long-term improvement
– linked to practical, 'do-able' activities at the school and classroom level
– relevant to adolescent learners.

Use practical strategies

Strategies for effective learning in middle and secondary schools incorporate literacy and subject area emphases. For learning to be purposeful, and for the secondary achievement 'dip' to be arrested, the strategies that teachers adopt cannot be chosen randomly or carelessly. Strategies need to be selected by:

– careful planning based on pupils' needs. The planning should incorporate motivation, challenge and support that enables them to tackle the literacy demands of subject areas
– discriminating precisely the match between strategies and the likelihood that they will assist progress towards particular outcomes or objectives (some strategies, for example, promote reading, others target writing objectives).

Work on a variety of fronts

Improving learning for adolescent pupils requires a continuing effort over time, and in a variety of areas. Individual teachers contribute a lot to the improvement effort. Their task is made so much easier if the organisation, culture and support within the school are 'in synch' with what they are trying to achieve.

Expand the repertoire

Strong pressures have acted in concert to narrow the instructional response to the needs of adolescent learners. To improve learning, the repertoire of responses needs to be expanded to include consideration of a variety of:

– school organisational arrangements
– within school support models for literacy
– learning, teaching and assessment strategies.

An extended repertoire will enable pupils to acquire literacy and learning skills within subject content. Improved skills will result in:

– more effective processing of information
– greater understanding of subject content
– better learning outcomes.

The Stepping Out *approach*

The role of teachers

Pupils in the middle and secondary school context spend most of their time with mainstream teachers. These teachers know their pupils, and know their subject well. This is their area of expertise. Subject area teachers are therefore the people best placed to support pupils to tackle the literacy demands of their learning area. This does not mean that they need to become literacy teachers instead of subject teachers. It means that if teachers are familiar with a wide range of strategies that can be put in place to help pupils more effectively learn subject area content, then their teaching, and pupils' learning outcomes, will improve in all subject areas.

The *Stepping Out* philosophy is that no individual or department can be held responsible for improving all pupils' literacy skills in all learning areas. English departments have as many obligations as other teachers to meet the requirements of school, system and national mandates. The responsibility for literacy improvement is therefore one shared by all teachers in a department and across the school. This does not necessarily mean a 'language across the curriculum approach', but a 'curriculum literacies approach that builds up the learning tools within each learning area, and helps pupils to tackle the demands of the different subject areas.

The need for support

Secondary teachers frequently express anxiety about the fact that increasing numbers of their pupils require support with their reading and writing. They also express doubts about their own ability to be able adequately to provide such support. A significant number feel that their pre-service training equipped them to teach the content of their subject, but that it did not necessarily provide them with the skills, understandings and strategies required to help pupils who need individual and specific instruction in reading and writing. They therefore have limited understandings about the literacy demands of their learning area, limited understandings about intervention strategies and limited understandings of how to monitor pupils' learning outcomes effectively. This makes it extremely difficult for them to put in place strategies that will effectively enhance pupils' learning outcomes. Teachers need practical and sustained support to take up this important role.

The skills required to teach literacy effectively are not hard to learn. Secrets about teaching literacy are *not* confined to an elite group of teachers. It is true, though, that some training and knowledge are required. Professional development programmes such as *Stepping Out* build on teachers' skills and knowledge, and support teachers as they work to improve pupils' learning outcomes. It is essential that schools ensure that all teachers receive professional training that gives them the skills and understandings (and the confidence) to help all pupils to make progress.

Stepping Out as an intervention

Stepping Out is a multifaceted literacy improvement resource. It was developed specifically for the tricky terrain of the middle and secondary school context. It is in this phase that pupils can be difficult, that organisational structures and timetable can be inflexible, where the literacy demands of different subject areas become increasingly more complex, and where it becomes difficult to make links between learning areas.

The resource directly addresses issues related to the context within which middle and secondary school learning occurs. It targets teachers' needs and gives them the skills and confidence required to help pupils to tackle the literacy demands of their learning area. *Stepping Out* also acknowledges and builds on teachers' skills and understandings about teaching, learning and assessment. It aims to improve pupils' learning outcomes – in all learning areas.

The four elements of *Stepping Out*

Stepping Out comprises four elements:

— Professional development and training
— School development planning
— Teaching and learning strategies
— Curriculum support materials.

Uses of *Stepping Out*

Stepping Out can be implemented in small or large steps, depending on what teachers, departments and schools can manage. For example, it can be used to build on the skills and understandings of individual and/or groups of teachers. Alternatively, it can be used to provide a vehicle for whole school, LEA or educational systems reform. The degree of implementation depends on how the teachers and the leaders in each school perceive the needs in their particular context.

BENEFITS OF *STEPPING OUT*

Whole School, Staff, Groups of Schools, LEAs

Provides LEAs with a strategy for supporting schools

Enables school wide approaches to literacy to be developed

Focuses school planning

Establishes priorities for professional development

Collects information towards accountability for performance

Teachers, Small Groups, Teams, Subject Departments

Assists collaboration between teachers and subject departments

Supports a culture of innovation and improvement

Provides ideas and materials for learning, teaching and assessment at the classroom level

Builds on and extends expertise, skills and understandings

Assists planning processes

Enables common goals and a consistent approach to literacy to be developed

Tutors

Extends knowledge and understandings about the role of literacy

Builds skills of facilitation, collaboration and coaching of other teachers

Provides training as Change Agents

Provides training to monitor literacy programmes

Professional development overview

The *Stepping Out* Tutor training course program consists of a two day module in Writing, a two day module in Reading/Viewing and a one day Tutor course that prepares Tutors to act as Change Agent within their particular context. Tutors are provided with a range of ideas for managing whole school and/or subject area plans for literacy improvement. They are also provided with practical suggestions for implementing *Stepping Out* strategies within cross-curriculum, subject specific content.

Two day *Stepping Out* classroom teacher courses will become available at a later date. These courses will focus on Writing, or Reading/Viewing.

A third, two-day module in Listening/Speaking/Thinking, and Curriculum Issues will also become available at a later date.

These additional courses and modules will be advertised locally once they are available.

An overview of the five day Tutor training program follows:

Stepping Out tutor training course

Time	Writing Module		Reading/Viewing Module		Tutor Training
	Monday	Tuesday	Wednesday	Thursday	Friday
9 am	Learning in the Middle and Secondary School	Written Genres	What Matters in Reading and Viewing	Selecting Texts for the Middle and Secondary School	The Role of the Tutor as a Change Agent
11 am	Morning Tea	Morning Tea	Morning Tea	Morning Tea	Morning Tea
11:20 am	Monitoring Pupils' Writing	A Problem Solving Approach to Writing	Applying a Reading and Viewing Framework	↓ Top Level Structures and Note-making Frameworks	Subject Area and Whole School Planning
1 pm	Lunch	Lunch	Lunch	Lunch	Lunch
1:45 pm	↓ Subject Specific Spelling	Journal Writing in Subject Areas / Implementing Writing	↓ An Introduction to Critical Literacy	↓ Implementing Reading/Viewing	↓ Issues and Concerns
4:30 pm	Finish	Finish	Finish	Finish	Finish

Conclusion

The Middle Years of schooling should be so busy, so demanding, so active, so adventurous, so spectacular that young adolescents should barely have time for brooding introspection or watching Australian soap operas. They should learn, in the Middle Years, not only about the academic curriculum but also about how to relate to and work with others. They should learn that education and learning are not separate from life, but integral to it. As they get older, they should see learning, work and leisure being woven into a single plait, in which the three separate strands are identifiable, but also united, to give strength, pattern and purpose …

(Barber, 1999)

We should make their heads spin …

SECTION TWO

Literacy and Learning Strategies

6 Stepping Out strategies

Why strategies?

The *Stepping Out* teaching and learning strategies contained in this text are a compilation of tried and tested, cross-curricular strategies that are recognised as being representative of successful teaching and learning practices. All of the strategies assist teachers in addressing the literacy and learning needs of their pupils. They are not unique to the *Stepping Out* programme but are based on the work of many researchers, including Halliday (1973), Martin (1985), Morris and Stewart-Dore (1984), Bruner (1986), and Vygotsky (1986).

Included are:

- a range of strategies that facilitate learning in all subject areas
- examples of literacy strategies incorporated within subject specific content
- concept and skill strategies
- indications of the purpose of each strategy
- the methods of implementing each strategy
- the behaviours to look for when monitoring pupils' processes and products
- ways to collect data.

A *Stepping Out* premise is that, once target learning objectives have been determined and teachers have identified pupils' placement in relation to the targets, strategies can then be put in place to support or extend their learning. When teachers are familiar with the ways in which particular strategies work and the types of learning they facilitate, they are able to select those strategies that help pupils to make progress from one level of learning to another. They are also able to determine:

- who needs support
- what kind of support would be appropriate
- when to remove, modify or replace the support (scaffolding) strategy.

As pupils make progress, the support strategies (scaffolding) can be removed or replaced. The aim is to enable pupils to be aware of the ways in which these strategies can help them to learn more effectively, and to self-select and apply them confidently in different contexts and for different purposes.

Introducing strategies in the classroom

Strategies need to be explicitly explained and modelled several times before pupils can apply them independently. They need to know *how* to apply, and *when* and *where* to apply them. They also need to have multiple opportunities to practise and develop them so that they become tools for learning. The steps to independence are illustrated in the diagram on p.40.

In a strategies-rich classroom, it is useful to teach one or two strategies and to build up the repertoire slowly. Strategies can be explicitly taught and modelled in both small and large group instruction and in one-to-one teaching situations. Explicit explanations, modelling, guidance and feedback should continue as pupils practise using the strategies.

Instructions should explain when and where to apply the strategies, as well as explain the benefits associated with using various strategies. Pupils can be prompted (through questioning techniques) to think about additional or possible ways to extend and expand their use of strategies. The ways in which different pupils apply strategies to the same content can be highlighted and individual pupils can explain why (and how) they used a particular strategy to complete a piece of work (Pressley, 2000).

Selecting appropriate strategies

Great care needs to be taken when selecting strategies. The strategies incorporated in this text are not designed to be used in a 'grab bag' fashion. Some support learning. Some provide organisational structures. Others facilitate comprehension. Each suits different kinds of tasks and achieves different purposes. Some are flexible and can be used equally well at *before*, *during* or *after* stages of a lesson or unit of work. Teachers should use their professional judgement to identify which strategies will ensure that pupils achieve targeted learning outcomes. The inappropriate selection of strategies can enhance or detract from learning experiences.

WARNING

The indiscriminate use of the strategies in this text can be hazardous to learning!

Concepts and skills

Pupils do not learn *skills* and *concepts* in the same way. Strategies that support the teaching of skills and concepts therefore differ, according to whether a skill or concept is to be taught.

Concepts are best taught by building up layers of understanding, starting from the knowledge that pupils already possess. As new knowledge is assimilated, new understandings are able to be formed. Strategies suitable for teaching concepts allow pupils to move between overall generalisations and details, and to explore links between subject specific information and their own world.

Examples of strategies that facilitate the teaching of concepts

Three level guides	which promote critical thinking and internalisation of concepts.
Journal writing	which facilitates reflection and recording of understandings.
Group work	which provides opportunities for active participation in clarifying and refining ideas.
For, against and questions	which facilitate synthesis of other points of view on a topic.

Skills, on the other hand, need to be explicitly taught. Strategies, such as *modelling* the skill, and collaborative activities, such as *guided writing* and *joint construction*, are very effective. It is important to determine how many subskills are involved in each task and to identify the order and rate at which these subskills should be taught.

Examples of strategies that facilitate the teaching of skills

Joint construction	where the teacher and pupils collaboratively construct a piece of writing, such as a letter, a limerick or a report.
Guided writing	where the linguistic (language) features and conventions of a text are made clear through modelling.
Skimming	where pupils are explicitly taught how to gain a general impression or overview of the content of a text.
Scanning	where pupils are explicitly taught how to locate specific details quickly, such as names or dates.

Using a planning framework

The *before, during* and *after* framework is an adaptation of the ERICA reading framework (Morris and Stewart-Dore, 1984). It is an extremely effective model to use when planning a learning programme. The framework supports teachers as they:

– *prepare* pupils for tasks
– provide support strategies that help pupils to *think through* and *organise their ideas* during tasks
– determine ways in which pupils can *demonstrate their understandings*.

Before, During and After Framework		
BEFORE (What will you do to *prepare* pupils for the task?)	**Background information**	*Select strategies which:* – activate background knowledge – link existing knowledge to new information – review, extend, enrich and clarify vocabulary and concepts
	Awareness of purpose	*Select strategies which:* – motivate pupils' interest – establish a purpose for the activity
DURING (How will you help pupils to *think through* and *organise* ideas?)	**Thinking through**	*Select strategies which enable pupils to:* – think through ideas – self-monitor their understandings
	Organising	*Select strategies which help pupils to:* – extract and organise relevant information for a specific task
AFTER (How will you get pupils to *demonstrate or translate* their understanding?)	**Using new information**	*Select strategies which enable pupils to:* – evaluate ideas critically – demonstrate understanding of learning

When *planning* a learning activity or programme, teachers should do the following:

1. Start at the ***after*** stage, to determine:

    – the target learning objectives
    – how pupils could best demonstrate these target learning objectives.

2. Then move to the ***before*** stage, to determine:

    – where pupils are placed in relation to the target objectives/outcomes
    – how to bridge the gap between their existing knowledge and the new knowledge to be learned
    – strategies which would best facilitate pupils' understandings and mastery of new vocabulary
    – whether there are concepts, skills or sets of subskills to be learned, and how best to teach these
    – how to link the learning to real-life, authentic contexts.

3. Plan the ***during*** section, to determine:

    – the kinds of support strategies that will enable pupils to think through the activity and to organise their thinking (i.e. three level guides, directed silent reading, retrieval charts, etc.)
    – the type of assessment that could be integrated within the process.

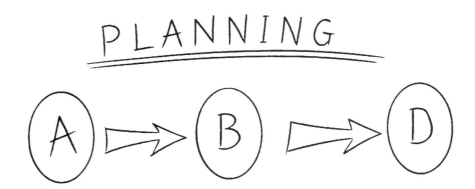

Using the framework for planning		
1	**AFTER (Demonstrating)**	**What are the target learning objectives?** What understandings/skills do I want pupils to demonstrate? How could they best show this?
2	**BEFORE (Preparing)**	**Where are my pupils placed with respect to the target learning objectives?** What do they already know? What else do they need to know? What task or strategies will enable them to build on their existing knowledge? What strategies could be used to teach the concepts, skills or subskills involved in this task/lesson/unit?
3	**DURING (Engaging)**	**What key points/concepts will pupils need to learn?** What support will they need to do this? How could they organise their information? Which strategies would be useful? What type of assessment could be integrated within the process (i.e. ongoing observational notes, check-lists, self-evaluation forms, etc.)?

Teaching from the framework

- When using the framework in the classroom, start from the *before* stage and move through the *during* and *after* stages.

- It is not necessary, and it is too time consuming, to plan *before, during* and *after* activities for each and every lesson. Some strategies are best used at the *before* or *during* stage of a learning programme. Others can be used effectively at any stage of the learning process. Choice is determined by the purpose of the activity and the needs of pupils.

- Time invested in *before* and *during* activities leads to an improvement in the quality of pupils' learning outcomes, and is therefore time well spent.

A useful sequence of strategies for a classroom lesson could look like this:

BEFORE *Prepare pupils for the learning that lies ahead*	• Brainstorm ideas, or • Provide an anticipation guide, or • Provide an overview of the unit or lesson
DURING *Provide scaffolding, so that pupils can think through their ideas and organise their information effectively*	• Jointly devise a retrieval chart, or • Use a framework so that pupils can record their research information, or • Provide a series of focus questions, or • Ask pupils to draw a 'mind map'
AFTER *Provide opportunities for pupils to demonstrate their understandings*	• Produce an oral report, or • Perform a group role-play, or • Write a persuasive argument, or • Report back to the class

General strategies

Each of the strategies listed below is described in detail on the following pages.

Strategies	B	D	A	Concept	Skill	Reading	Writing	Listening	Speaking	Page No.
Card Cluster	✓	✓	✓	✓	✓	✓	✓	✓	✓	102
Envoy		✓	✓	✓	✓	✓	✓	✓	✓	106
For, Against and Questions			✓	✓			✓			110
Jigsaw		✓	✓	✓		✓	✓	✓	✓	114
Modelling	✓	✓	✓		✓		✓	✓	✓	116
Pupil Generated Questions		✓	✓	✓	✓					118
Rotating Groups or Papers		✓	✓	✓		✓	✓	✓	✓	122
Small Group Work	✓	✓	✓	✓	✓			✓	✓	126

Card Cluster

What is its purpose?

- To collate ideas discussed at the small group level effectively

- To teach pupils to distinguish between main ideas and supporting detail

- To teach pupils how to organise ideas

- To provide opportunities for pupils to support and develop their ideas

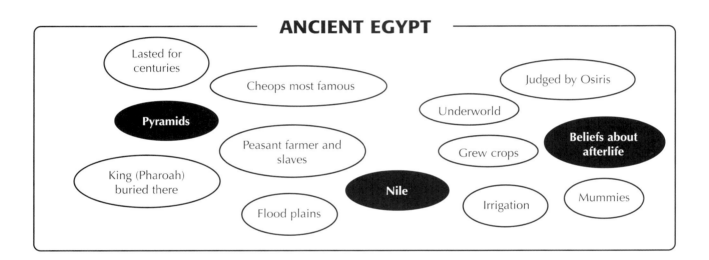

ANCIENT EGYPT

Lasted for centuries — Cheops most famous — Pyramids — Peasant farmer and slaves — King (Pharoah) buried there — Flood plains — Nile — Judged by Osiris — Underworld — Grew crops — Beliefs about afterlife — Irrigation — Mummies

How can I implement it?

- Distribute several cards and a thick pen to each small group.

- Explain the purpose of the exercise, i.e. to generate and then organise ideas on a topic.

- Provide clear directions of what is to be recorded.

- Ensure only key words are clearly recorded on cards.

- Ask one group member to pin up his or her group's cards so that related ideas are clustered together.

- Ask other groups' representatives, one at a time, to cluster their cards. New ideas are placed in a new space, same ideas on top of previously pinned card, and cards related to pinned card are placed near the appropriate card. Pupils may be asked to justify their arrangement of cards.

What am I looking for? (Evaluation)

Examples of some of the skills/understandings that may be observed include:

- the extent of subject understandings;
- the ability to generate ideas;
- the ability to organise information meaningfully;
- the ability to select key words and phrases;
- the ability to distinguish between main ideas and supporting detail;
- the level of metacognition:
  - the extent to which pupils know when it is useful to use a card cluster;
  - the extent to which pupils apply the strategy independently;
  - the extent to which the strategy is applied to appropriate contexts;
- the ability to support and develop ideas.

How can I collect information?
– Formative and Summative Evaluation

METHOD	EXAMPLE
Pupil evaluation Peer evaluation Teacher jottings On balance judgements Criteria check-lists Anecdotal information Parent input Portfolio	**Teacher jottings** 'Anthony can generate ideas but has difficulty seeing the relationships between ideas.' **Criteria check-list –** **Observation at the small group level**

CRITERIA	PUPILS' NAMES			
Ability to generate ideas				
Ability to distinguish between main idea and supporting detail				
Ability to organise information meaningfully				

Pupil evaluation
'At first I couldn't understand why the other groups clustered their ideas in the way they did. But when I listened to their explanations it gradually became clearer. I understand the topic really well now.'

Card Cluster examples

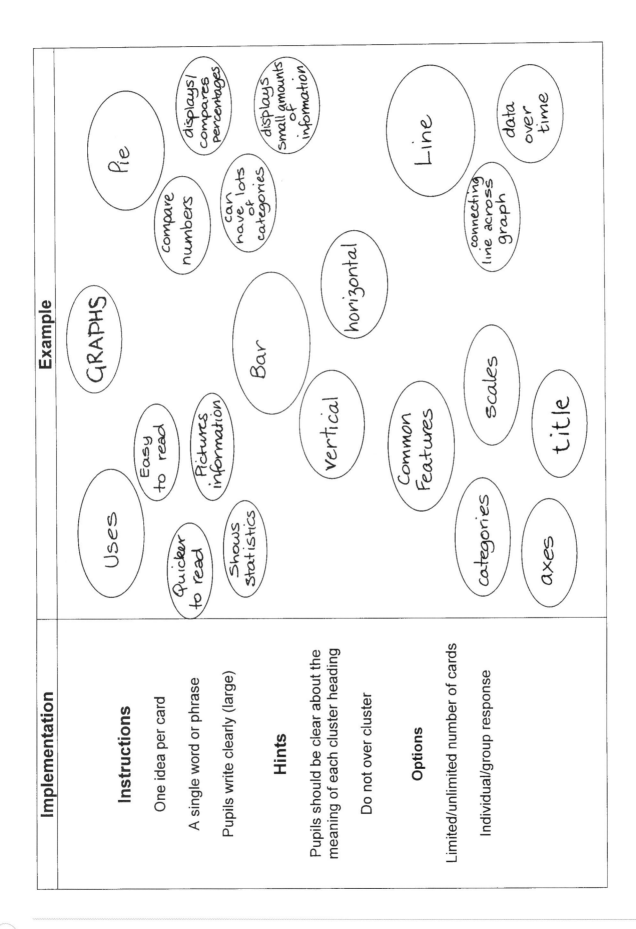

Example

GRAPHS

Pie
- displays/compares percentages
- displays small amounts of information
- compare numbers
- can have lots of categories

Line
- data over time
- connecting line across graph

Uses
- Easy to read
- Pictures information
- Quicker to read
- Shows Statistics

Bar
- horizontal
- vertical

Common Features
- scales
- title
- categories
- axes

Implementation

Instructions

One idea per card

A single word or phrase

Pupils write clearly (large)

Hints

Pupils should be clear about the meaning of each cluster heading

Do not over cluster

Options

Limited/unlimited number of cards

Individual/group response

Stepping Out *A Whole School Approach to Literacy* This material is not copyright free.

Implementation

Example

Rocks

Igneous
- Cooling molten material
- basalt
- roods
- paving
- building blocks
- granite
- table tops
- headstones

Metamorphic
- heat and pressure
- slate
- roof tiles
- floor tiles
- floor / wall tiles
- marble
- statues

Sedimentary
- concrete
- limestone
- cement
- layers of sediment
- beaches
- river beds
- lake beds
- ocean beds

Instructions

One idea per card

A single word or phrase

Pupils write clearly (large)

Hints

Pupils should be clear about the meaning of each cluster heading

Do not over cluster

Options

Limited/unlimited number of cards

Individual/group response

Envoy

What is its purpose?

- To provide a structure and accountability to group discussions

- To encourage pupils to learn from each other and take responsibility for learning

- To develop listening and oral skills

- To promote skills in synthesising and summarising

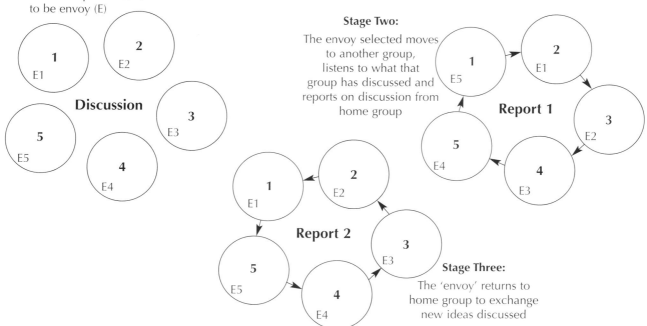

Stage One:
Each group discusses the topic and chooses a representative to be envoy (E)

Discussion

Stage Two:
The envoy selected moves to another group, listens to what that group has discussed and reports on discussion from home group

Report 1

Report 2

Stage Three:
The 'envoy' returns to home group to exchange new ideas discussed

How can I implement it?

- Pupils are formed into groups and each group is given the same topic to discuss or research.

- One pupil from each group is selected to be the 'envoy'.

- After the completion of discussion or research each envoy reports to another group and outlines what was discussed – what ideas or suggestions were made, what conclusions were reached, what decisions were made, etc.

- The envoy listens to ideas discussed in the group that he or she is visiting.

- The envoy returns to the original or home group and exchanges with their group members any new ideas.

What am I looking for? (Evaluation)

Examples of some of the skills/understandings that may be observed include:

- the ability to summarise and synthesise ideas;
- the ability to organise information clearly;
- the level of pupils' background knowledge;
- the level of understanding of concepts discussed;
- the ability to listen effectively;
- the extent to which pupils critically question and reflect on ideas.

How can I collect information?
– Formative and Summative Evaluation

METHOD	EXAMPLE
Pupil evaluation Peer evaluation Teacher jottings On balance judgements Criteria check-lists Anecdotal information Parent input Portfolio	**Peer evaluation** 'Robin reported on her group's discussion. She explained their ideas clearly. All of us understood what she said because she organised her ideas logically and gave us examples for each idea.' **Teacher jottings** 'The pupils in Sam's group were listening very intently. They synthesised effectively what the envoy said.' **Anecdotal information** 'More opportunities to summarise and synthesise ideas needed. Over half the class had trouble.' **Criteria check-list**

CRITERIA	PUPILS' NAMES			
Summarised the main ideas effectively				
Organised ideas in report effectively				
Sound level of understandings				

Example of an Envoy topic

White Christmas turkey

ANDRÉ MALAN

Ho Ho Ho.... GOODWILL TO ALL MEN!!

THERE is a fairly good argument — the same one you would use to discourage George Grijusich from playing the Sugar Plum Fairy — why Myer should be entitled to exclude women from its annual Santa Claus school.

Santa Claus is a man. There is no doubt about that. In history, myth and tradition there has never been the slightest hint that the bewhiskered old sleigh pilot had anything other than the standard XY chromosome combination.

From their earliest days children are told all about *Father* Christmas, and you can imagine how it would confuse their tender minds if they went to a Myer store and found themselves sitting on the knee of a Santa with a high-pitched voice, big bosoms and nail polish that matched his jacket.

But I'm at a loss to understand why the retail giant also wanted its Santas to be as white as the driven snow. Apart from being racist, unnecessary and contrary to the Christmas spirit, this stipulation on Myer's Santa job description was also historically flawed, as I will explain later.

Myer had intended to appear before the Anti-Discrimination Tribunal in Melbourne yesterday to apply for an exemption from the Equal Opportunity Act so that it could legally employ only white male Santas.

But it withdrew its submission to the tribunal after protests that it was racist and discriminatory.

At first I thought the "whites only" statement was a joke or a publicity stunt, but the Myer people solemnly insisted that they sought the ruling because they wanted only traditional and authentic Santas.

In South Africa not too many years ago they used to have something called the Race Classification Board which was charged with the responsibility of determining whether people were white enough to enjoy privileged health care, education, housing and job opportunities.

They used to examine the colour of the applicant's skin, the shape of his or her nose, lips, eyes etc. They even had one test in which they inserted a comb in the hair. If the hair was fine enough for the comb to drop out, it improved your chances of being declared white, which in those days was akin to winning Lotto.

As soon as I read about Myer and its quest for Aryan Santas, I had visions of the company's human resources staff running combs through the hair of the nervous wannabe Santas.

In fact, if Myer wanted to be totally authentic, it would also have to reject fair-haired and fair-skinned applicants.

You see, like the man whose birth we celebrate at Christmas, the original Santa Claus was almost certainly a rather swarthy chap.

Santa Claus as he is imagined in Western countries these days is based on Sinterklaas, a Dutch variation of St Nicholas, which was taken to the American colonies in the 17th century by migrants from Holland.

But Sinterklaas, in turn, was based on St Nicholas, a minor saint who was born in the 4th century in Lycia, an ancient region on the coast of south-west Asia Minor, which had been under both Persian and Syrian rule. It's a region whose residents would probably have been too dark to pass the Myer Santa test.

Nicholas was a generous and kind man, and legends grew around the miracles he performed for the poor and unhappy. According to my encyclopaedia, he was reputed to have given marriage dowries of gold to three girls whom poverty would otherwise have forced into prostitution and he restored life to three children who had been chopped up by a butcher and put into a brine tub.

IN TIME a cult grew around the legend of St Nicholas, the remnants of which were taken to America by the Dutch and transformed into familiar ruddy cheeked and white bearded store Santas we have today.

From my experience children are blissfully unaware of racial differences and would be unperturbed if the face behind the whiskers was Asian, Aboriginal (think Burnum Burnum), or of any other race.

All they're really interested in is the presents he might bring them.

● Andre Malan is going on leave. His column will resume on October 14.

Myer retracts Santa clause

MELBOURNE

FATHER Christmas at Myer stores this year could in fact be Mother Christmas — or a man who does not conform to the traditional white stereotype.

Myer has abandoned its move to restrict its store Santa Clauses to white males only.

The store withdrew a submission to the Anti-Discrimination Tribunal yesterday, after protests that it was racist and discriminatory.

Managing director Terry McCartney said Myer was a commercial organisation that operated within the mores and laws of society.

"We have never sought to be the centre of a debate on the issue," he said.

"In making the application we did not mean to offend. If we did offend anyone, on either side of the debate, then we apologise."

Mr McCartney said Myer's recruiting procedures for the position would apply the store's present policy of non-discrimination on the basis of sex or race.

It was too early to say how many, if any, women or non-white Santas would be employed.

Asked what the attitude of children would be to a non-traditional Father Christmas, Mr McCartney said: "That will be interesting — they are a primary concern in all of this."

But based on the views of the adult community, some would have a "very stereotyped or traditional view" and others would have a different point of view.

Stop messing with our Santa

THE row over Myer's decision — since reversed — to employ only elderly, white males as Santa Clauses, demonstrates an interesting paradox.

Those who preach tolerance seem to be intolerant of anyone who does not share their view.

The traditional Santa Claus is part of my culture. I submit that multiculturalism means accepting and embracing all cultures and creeds with equality, tolerance and respect. It does not mean forcing one culture to change its traditions to accommodate another.

Yet here we have the white, Anglo-Saxon, Christian culture, which represents the majority of Australia, having to accommodate those who do not fall within its ambit.

If any other culture was subjected to this it would be called racism.

Santa Claus is associated with the celebration of the birth of Christ and is therefore implicitly associated with benevolence, charity and good will to all people.

It is by no means a racist, sexist, or religiously discriminatory tradition. Quite the contrary. But it is a tradition nonetheless.

Christians are conscious of, and sensitive to, the cultures and beliefs of other creeds. Have they not the right to preserve their culture too?

To change the appearance of Santa Claus to appease a few "political correctness" activists seems to me to be politicising something that was not meant to be political.

The question is not whether a black person or a woman could play Santa Claus. The question is whether they should.

D R LOVE Mullaloo

Some Critical Questions

Read the collection of articles silently and discuss the following focus questions in groups of four. You will be expected to provide feedback at the class level.   :

- Outline the situation described in the texts.

- Whose interests are represented by the traditional Father Christmas ?

- Whose interests are ignored?

- What other issues can you identify in the articles?

- Do you believe that it would be more politically correct to change the age, gender, culture or appearance of Father Christmas ? Why?

- What solutions would you offer for a multicultural nation such as ours?

For, Against and Questions

What is its purpose?

- To provide a framework for exploring an issue
- To teach pupils to consider different points of view

Issue: _____

For		Against

Questions:

How can I implement it?

- Explain the purpose of the activity.

- Explain the meanings of headings on the chart (*For, Against and Questions*). Point out that what one group sees as a *for* may be viewed as an *against* by another group.

- Pupils in pairs, or small groups, list as many ideas as they can in the time provided. *Questions* can be generated and recorded.

- Collate ideas discussed at the small group level through a call-out or by groups clustering ideas written on cards.

- Discuss pupil generated questions at the whole class level.

- The *For, Against and Questions* Chart may then serve as a framework for pupils' writing.

What am I looking for? (Evaluation)

Examples of some of the skills/understandings that may be observed include:

- the extent to which pupils consider others' points of view;
- the extent to which pupils analyse an issue critically;
- the level of metacognition:
  - the extent to which pupils can explain the value of the strategy;
  - the extent to which pupils apply the strategy independently to appropriate different contexts.

How can I collect information?
– Formative and Summative Evaluation

METHOD	EXAMPLE
Pupil evaluation Peer evaluation Teacher jottings On balance judgements Criteria check-lists Anecdotal information Parent input Portfolio	**Teacher jottings** 'Ellis, Karl, and Tuan worked really well using their *For, Against and Questions* Chart. They were able to consider different points of view. They knew about the issues.' **Anecdotal information** 'In Health Education the teacher tells me Nicole suggested using a *For and Against* Chart to explore an issue in class. She showed him the strategy and all pupils then used it.' **Parent input** 'You know how hard Neil finds it to organise his ideas and keep focused? Well, that *For and Against* Chart you set for homework worked really well. He gained a real sense of satisfaction from finishing a piece of work.'

For, Against and Questions examples

LOCKIE'S RELATIONSHIPS WITH OTHERS

	FOR	AGAINST	QUESTIONS
Family			
School			
Vicki			
Peer Group			
Bogans			
Church Group			

Reference: Winton, T. (1990), *Lockie Leonard, Human Torpedo*, Puffin Books

Static Electricity

FOR

- Many inventions use static electricity
- Use in photocopies
- Use in air filters

AGAINST

- Zaps when you rub on things like a car door or trampoline
- Clothes stick, so fabric softener has to be used
- Flashes of lightning are dangerous – they can cause fires
- Dust sticks to the television and computer screen

QUESTIONS

Are there only two kinds of charges?

What kinds of materials attract or repel?

Why do objects attract or repel each other?

Jigsaw

What is its purpose?

- To provide a structure for small group work
- To encourage participative, co-operative learning and to place responsibility for learning on the pupil
- To cover a broad amount of information economically

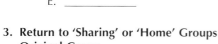

Topic: _____

Aspects
A. _____
B. _____
C. _____
D. _____
E. _____

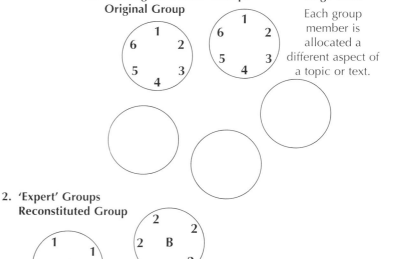

1. 'Sharing' or 'Home' Groups
Original Group

Stage One:
Each group member is allocated a different aspect of a topic or text.

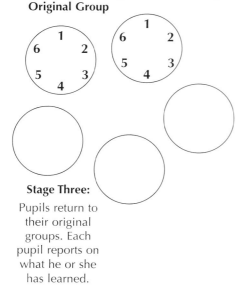

3. Return to 'Sharing' or 'Home' Groups
Original Group

Stage Three:
Pupils return to their original groups. Each pupil reports on what he or she has learned.

2. 'Expert' Groups
Reconstituted Group

Stage Two:
Group members reform so that they all have the same aspect of the topic about which to become expert.

How can I implement it?

- Pupils are formed into 'sharing' or 'home' groups, e.g. five groups of six. Each pupil is given a number (1–6).

- Every member of the 'home' group has a different aspect of a topic to discuss/research.

- Each 'number' moves to a particular group that explores one aspect of a topic. This newly formed group becomes an 'expert' group.

- Pupils research their aspect of the topic in the 'expert' groups and prepare to report to their 'home' group.

- Pupils move back to their original 'home' groups.

- Pupils take turns to report as the 'expert' on their aspect of the topic. Others in the groups can take notes.

What am I looking for? (Evaluation)

Examples of some of the skills/understandings that may be observed include:

- the level of pupil understanding;
- the level of engagement in the activity;
- the extent to which subject specific vocabulary is embedded;
- the ability critically to analyse, evaluate and apply ideas;
- the ability to support their ideas;
- the ability to summarise and synthesise main ideas.

How can I collect information?
– Formative and Summative Evaluation

METHOD	EXAMPLE
Pupil evaluation Peer evaluation Teacher jottings On balance judgements Criteria check-lists Anecdotal information Parent input Portfolio	**Pupil evaluation** 'I learned a lot about probability through today's jigsaw. I found it really helpful to ask questions of the rest of the group.' **Criteria check-list**

CRITERIA	PUPILS' NAMES			
Understood the main ideas				
Displayed evidence of subject specific vocabulary embedded in classroom language				
Displayed ability to support and develop ideas				

Anecdotal information
'Chris's English teacher confirmed my judgement that his ability to express himself orally is improving. Today in a jigsaw activity he summarised the group's discussion clearly and succinctly'.

Modelling

What is its purpose?

- To make explicit the cognitive processes and skills that learners go through when they complete a task (showing by example)

How can I implement it?

- Start slowly and choose a process or strategy that you feel comfortable to model (e.g. how to extract key words and phrases, how to generate ideas for an assignment through brainstorming, how to guess the meaning of a word in context). A range of suggestions is provided on the next page.

- In front of the whole class 'think aloud' to make explicit the cognitive processes required to complete the task successfully (while writing on the board, or on an overhead).

- If necessary seek support from colleagues such as the Special Needs Teacher in order to increase your range of learning strategies that can be modelled.

- Aim to promote metacognition by creating situations where pupils model skills for each other.

Examples of skills and strategies teachers and peers can model

- Steps for completing a homework task
- How to access particular information in the library
- How to solve a problem
- How to construct a paragraph
- How to ask for clarification
- How to listen effectively
- How to read maps or graphs
- How to write in a particular text form
- How to generate a note-making framework
- How to work co-operatively with other pupils
- How to edit
- How to write an effective topic sentence/paragraph
- How to set out references in a bibliography
- How to set out direct speech
- How to conduct a writers' conference
- How to reread to check whether the language is appropriate for purpose and audience
- How to combine simple sentences
- How to use a journal for different purposes
- How to complete a concept map (or other diagram)
- How to generate subheadings when making notes
- How to read around a word for context clues
- How to decide when to use a table of contents and/or an index
- How to develop and support ideas
- How to select an appropriate text form
- How to skim a chapter
- How to resolve conflict at the small group level
- How to generate ideas for writing
- How to study for a test

Pupil Generated Questions

What is their purpose?

- To provide practice for improving both the quality and the type of questions a reader asks

- To promote active meaning-making (prediction, thinking ideas through, substantiation, etc.)

- To promote pupil-centred learning (allows pupils to set their own purpose(s) for reading) and build interest in a topic

- To provide the teacher with instant feedback about areas of difficulty in the text

How can I implement them?

- Pupils generate questions about a topic in a variety of contexts. For example:
  - before the text is opened, pupils may list questions they want to know about the topic;
  - after silently reading the text, pupils may jot down the question that is most concerning them. Pupils, in small groups or pairs, help each other to discover the answer from the text by searching the text. Unresolved questions can be treated at the whole group level;
  - after comprehending a text, pupils construct a question about an aspect of the topic they want to pursue.

- Where appropriate, unresolved questions can be raised at the whole class level, and answered by other pupils and/or the teacher who can model referring to the text to substantiate ideas.

- The teacher is freed from the front of the class, and monitors individuals' and groups' comprehension skills and intervenes supportively at the small group level.

What am I looking for? (Evaluation)

Examples of some of the skills/understandings that may be observed include:

- the level of understanding of subject content and concepts;
- the quality of the questions pupils ask;
- the willingness of pupils to take risks;
- the level of pupils' critical thinking skills;
- the degree to which pupils are able to refer closely to the text to substantiate their interpretation;
- the extent to which pupils can develop and support their ideas;
- the extent to which pupils can use context clues to guess meaning.

How can I collect information?
– Formative and Summative Evaluation

METHOD	EXAMPLE
Pupil evaluation Peer evaluation Teacher jottings On balance judgements Criteria check-lists Anecdotal information Parent input Portfolio	**Peer evaluation** 'I found it very helpful to be able to ask my own questions and I also enjoyed helping others to find the answers. I also realised how important it is to go back to the text to justify your ideas.' **On balance judgements** 'Andrew's group (Michael, Tom and Chris) generated questions on forces that showed they had a deep understanding of the topic.' **Anecdotal information** 'More opportunities to summarise and synthesise ideas needed. Over half the class had trouble.' **Criteria check-list**

CRITERIA	PUPILS' NAMES			
Able to explain the main ideas in own words				
Able to explain how meaning was made				
Able to substantiate interpretation by close reference to the text				

Pupil Generated Questions examples

The Planets

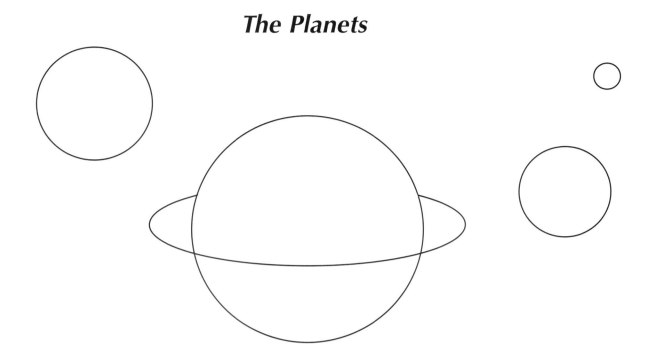

- Provide a box of texts on the subject of the planets.

- Ask the pupils to reflect on the topic and to list a number of questions they would like answered on the topic.
  e.g. What is a planet?
  How many are there?
  How were they formed?
  What are they made of?
  Which is closest to the Earth?
  Which is the biggest? The smallest?
  Is there life on any of the planets?

- Pupils share their questions at the small group level. They prioritise five key questions and read the texts provided, in order to find answers to their questions.

- Unanswered questions are referred to the whole class and answered at that level.

- Pupils can be encouraged to find answers to their questions on the Internet, or from alternative sources.

Topic: Fashion

Pupil generated questions.

- Who are some of the worlds leading designers of men's clothing? Women's clothing?
- What countries set the trends in fashion? Why?
- How have men's and women's fashion trends changed over the last fifty years?
- Why does men's clothing cost less than women's clothing?
- Why aren't men as fashion conscious as women?
- When did trousers become a fashionable choice for women?

Topic: Hemp

Pupil generated questions.

- Is hemp the same as marijuana?
- Does it have medicinal properties?
- How many other uses does it have?
- Can you smoke a hemp plant?
- In what countries is hemp a legal product?
- How is hemp fibre produced?
- Is hemp clothing better than cotton?

Rotating Groups or Papers

What is its purpose?

- To allow several issues or aspects of a topic to be covered efficiently

- To promote pupil-centred, collaborative problem solving

- To provide opportunities for revision of concepts

- To encourage critical thinking

Topic: Social Problems in Urban Areas

Group One			Group Two			Group Three			Group Four		
Crime			*Social Isolation*			*Poverty*			*Housing*		
Problems:			Problems:			Problems:			Problems:		
Causes	Solutions		Causes	Solutions		Causes	Solutions		Causes	Solutions	

How can I implement it?

- Each group is allocated an issue or aspect of a topic. Ideas are recorded on a large sheet of paper attached to a wall.

- After a set amount of time each group rotates clockwise to the next sheet of paper (a reporter may be left at each 'station' to talk through the issues/ideas recorded). The group at the next sheet of paper considers the ideas recorded and then adds any new ideas. (Where no reporter is left at each 'station', the visiting group may also be asked to indicate, with a tick, ideas they think are effective. A question mark can be placed next to ideas in need of clarification.) After about two minutes, the groups rotate again in the same direction to the next large sheet of paper and repeat the activity of considering the ideas, adding new ideas and perhaps indicating their reactions.

- Depending on the purpose of the activity, the groups may not need to rotate around all stations. Where pupils have recorded question marks, a discussion at the whole group level may be necessary.

- The activity may be an end in itself or may be preparation for a follow-up activity.

What am I looking for? (Evaluation)

Examples of some of the skills/understandings that may be observed include:

- the level of pupils' understandings;
- the extent to which pupils think critically;
- the extent to which pupils identify key issues;
- the extent to which pupils support and develop their ideas;
- the extent to which pupils work collaboratively.

How can I collect information?
– Formative and Summative Evaluation

METHOD	EXAMPLE
Pupil evaluation Peer evaluation Teacher jottings On balance judgements Criteria check-lists Anecdotal information Parent input Portfolio	**Peer evaluation** 'Group Two's chart showed they had really understood the causes and solutions of housing problems. They had several clearly explained reasons. Their chart helped me to understand the issue better.' **Criteria check-list**

CRITERIA	PUPILS' NAMES			
Displayed sound understanding of the issues				
Was able to develop and support ideas				
Clearly and logically organised his/her talk				

Example of Rotating Papers

Topic: The problem of homeless young people is a serious and worsening situation.

Group One	Group Two	Group Three	Group Four
Who is to blame?	What can be done to help them?	Who should be providing the help?	What can we do about the situation personally?

Process: Groups remain seated.

- Each group is issued a large sheet of paper. The focus (or question) is written at the top.

- All members brainstorm responses.

- At an allocated time (tap a spoon against a glass, or use a timing device), the papers are moved clockwise to the next groups.

- Once groups have their own paper returned, one member reports back at the whole class level.

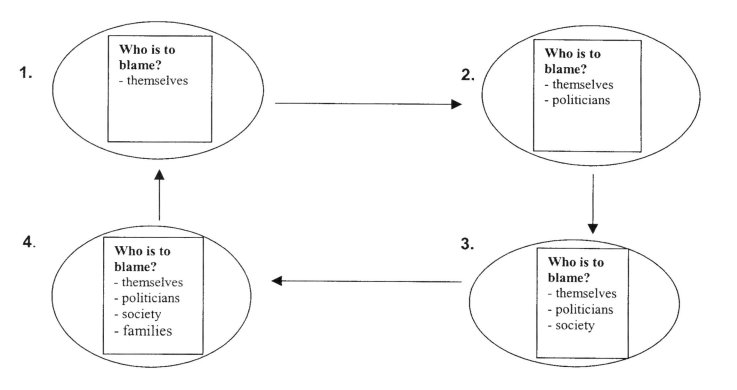

Teacher's notes

Topic: Homelessness

Activity: Rotating Papers

Issues: Group 1 – Who is to blame?
Group 2 – What can be done to help them?
Group 3 – Who should be providing the help?
Group 4 – What can we do about the situation personally?

Small Group Work

What is its purpose?

- To provide opportunities to learn through using language
- To clarify and extend ideas, and to practise language skills
- To embed subject specific vocabulary
- To create opportunities for peer teaching
- To develop co-operative learning skills

How can I implement it?

- Explain the purpose of the activity.
- Give clear directions about what is required.
- Set a specific time limit.
- Each group needs to appoint a timekeeper, a leader, a scribe for recording the 'group memory', and someone to 'feed back' information at the whole class level.
- Ensure pupils are accountable for their work, e.g. reporting back to the whole group (avoid needless repetition), reporting to another group, completing written work.
- Move around the groups to monitor each group in terms of the task being completed. (Is the group maintaining focus? Is the time required more or less?)
- Involve pupils in evaluating their co-operative learning skills.

What am I looking for? (Evaluation)

Examples of some of the skills/understandings that may be observed include:

- the level of pupils' understanding of concepts and content;
- the degree to which subject specific vocabulary is embedded in pupils' classroom language;
- the level of pupils' co-operative skills;
- the degree to which pupils think critically;
- the degree to which pupils synthesise information;
- the extent to which pupils apply their understandings to other contexts.

How can I collect information?
– Formative and Summative Evaluation

METHOD	EXAMPLE
Pupil evaluation Peer evaluation Teacher jottings On balance judgements Criteria check-lists Anecdotal information Parent input Portfolio	**Pupil evaluation** 'I worked quite well in my small group today. I kept to the topic and asked lots of good questions. What I need to work on is remembering not to dominate the discussion and to invite quieter members to give their opinions.' **On balance judgements** 'Antonio is learning to think far more critically now and is prepared to express his ideas at the small group level. Earlier in the year he wasn't comfortable giving his ideas.' **Criteria check-list**

CRITERIA	PUPILS' NAMES			
Showed sound understanding of concept				
Showed ability to apply understanding to different concepts				
Showed sound ability to synthesise ideas				

Examples of Small Group Work

GROUP SUMMARISING

Ask groups to read and summarise each paragraph of an article or text, by producing a single phrase that captures the essence of the paragraph. When all paragraphs have been treated this way, the phrases should present a summary of the story. Pupils need to discuss whether the final result captures the meaning of the original article or text.

SMALL GROUP DISCUSSION OF PART OF A TEXT

1. Provide a text and assign different sections of it for group members to read individually.

2. Pupils silently read their text, and then discuss what the section was about. The group comes up with a joint summary of the text content.

3. The teacher monitors the small group discussions in order to determine common areas of difficulty. These can be treated at the whole class level.

PICTURE BOOKS
(following exposure to a range of big books and picture books)

Pupils develop a picture book on a subject specific theme or concept. They work in groups with allocated roles: writer(s), researcher(s), illustrators, editor, and set timelines. The books may be suitable for sharing with others (local primary school, community library, etc.).

JOINT CREATION OF A WEBSITE OR PROMOTIONAL BROCHURE

Give groups the task of creating a website or brochure to publicise the school, or to publish the school newsletter, etc.

Vanessa awoke the next morning to the sounds of crying down stairs. She put on her slippers and slowly walked out of her room, fearing what might be the problem. She found her mother softly crying and her father trying to comfort her.

"Mum! Mum! What's wrong?"

Vanessa ran down the stairs as fast as she could, scared at what she might hear. She knew something bad had happened, but she couldn't think what it might be.

"Oh Vanessa, I have some terrible news, grandma isn't well, she's in hospital ," her mother answered, mumbling as she tried to say the words. Vanessa was stunned. She couldn't think straight. A pain of emotion and guilt came over her.

"Vanessa, sweetie, are you alright?"

Her father didn't know what to say, he was lost for words. Her mother was shocked and felt she was in another place, somewhere far away. Vanessa didn't utter a word. She ran back up the stairs into her bedroom, trying to escape the cold world. She lay on her bed burying her face in her warm pillow, letting all her emotions fall out.

"Noooo! Grandma!"

Examples of written work arising from small group discussion

7 References

Anthony R, Johnson T, Mickelson N, and Preece A, (1991), *Evaluating Literacy – A Perspective for Change*, Rigby Heinemann, Australia.

Barber, M. (1999), 'Taking the tide at the flood of transforming education in the middle years', Plenary Address, The Middle Years of Schooling Conference, Melbourne.

Barrett, R. (1998), Point and counterpoint. The future: The shape of middle schooling in Australia, *Curriculum Perspectives*, 18 (1).

Beane, J. (1990), A middle school curriculum from rhetoric to reality, *NMSA*, p.49.

Beane, J. (1991), The middle school: The natural home of the integrated curriculum, *Educational Leadership*, October, 49 (2), pp.9–13.

Beane, J. (1993), The search for a middle school curriculum, *The School Administrator*, 50 (3), pp.8–14.

Beane, J. (1995), Curriculum integration and the disciplines of knowledge,

Beane, J. and Brodhagen, B. (1995), Negotiating an integrated curriculum unit of study. What does the middle school curriculum look like? *The Middle Years Kit*, Videoconference at the ATC/NSN Middle Years Development School, Adelaide, April, 1995.

Berkley, G. (1994), Middle years of schooling – A Schools Council perspective, *Unicorn*, 20 (2), pp.5–11.

Bigum, C. and Green, B. (1993a), Aliens in the classroom, *Australian Journal of Education*, 37 (2), pp.119–141.

Bigum, C. and Green, B. (1993b), Technologizing literacy; or, interrupting the dream of reason. In P. Gilbert and A. Luke (Eds), *Literacy in Contexts: Australian Perspectives and Issues*, Allen & Unwin, Sydney, pp.4–28.

Brandes, D., Ginnis, P. and Hammond L. (1990), *The Student Centred School: Ideas for Practical Visionaries*, Blackwell Education, Oxford, p.13.

Brennan, M. and Sachs, J. (1998), *Curriculum, Classroom Materials for the Middle Years*, Australian Curriculum Studies Association, Canberra.

Bruner, J. (1986), *Actual Minds, Possible Worlds*, Cambridge University Press, London.

Cairney, T.H. (1992), 'Literacy for all: Exploding the myths of literacy', International Conference Committee, Australian Reading Association, Carlton, Victoria.

Cairney, T.H. and Ruge, J. (1996), 'Examining the impact of cultural mismatches between home and school: Coping with diversity in classrooms', Paper presented to American Association for Educational Research Conference, New York.

Cairney, T.H. and Ruge, J. (1997), *Community Literacy Practices and Schooling – Towards Effective Support for Students*, Executive summary, Department of Employment, Education, Training and Youth Affairs.

Cairney, T.H., Lowe K. and Sproats, E. (1995), *Literacy in Transition: An Investigation of the Literacy Practices of Upper Primary and Junior Secondary Schools*, vol. 1–3, D.E.E.T., Canberra.

Chapman, A. (1996), Current trends in language, literacy and classroom mathematics, Literacy and learning in mathematics, Curriculum support in mathemaics, *Stepping Out*, Education Department of Western Australia.

Clarke, J., Wideman, R. and Eadie, S. (1990), *Together We Learn – Co-Operative Small Group Learning*, Prentice-Hall, Canada, Inc., Scarborough, Ontario.

Comber, B. (1998), 'Literacies, contingent repertoires and school success', Garth Boomer Memorial Address, Joint National Conference of Australian ALEA and the ETA, Canberra.

Cross Curriculum Branch, *Stepping Out* (1997), Literacy and Learning Program, Years 6–10, Presenter's Files (No. 1 and 2). Education Department of Western Australia.

Cross Curriculum Branch, *Stepping Out Strategies Book* (1996), Education Department of Western Australia.

Cumming, J. (1994a), Educating young adolescents – An ASCA discussion paper, *Curriculum Perspectives*, Newsletter edition, November, pp.36–39.

Cumming, J. (1994b), Catering for the needs of all young adolescents: Towards an integrated approach, *Unicorn*, 20 (2), pp.12–20.

Cumming, J. (1996), *From Alienation to Engagement: Opportunities for Reform in the Middle Years of Schooling*, vol. 3, Australian Curriculum Studies Association, Belconnen, ACT.

Cumming, J. (1999), Into the community, An edited extract published in *Education Quarterly*, Issue 4, Summer, Curriculum Corporation, Melbourne, from *The Guide to Effective Community Based Learning*, Australian College of Education, PO Box 323, Deakin West, ACT 2600.

Cumming, J., Wyatt-Smith, C., Ryan, J. and Doig, S. (1998), *The Literacy-Curriculum Interface. The Literacy Demands of the Curriculum in Post-compulsory Schooling*, Executive summary, Department of Employment, Education, Training and Youth Affairs. Griffith University, ACT.

Curriculum Framework (1998), Curriculum Council, Western Australia.

Dimmock, C. (1993), University of Western Australia. Cited in D. Benda (1993), Flexibility is the key, *West Australian Newspaper*.

Earle, L. and Hargreaves, A. (1990), *Rights of Passage: A Review of Selected Research about Schools in the Transition Years*, Ontario Ministry for Education, Toronto.

Education Department of Western Australia, *Stepping Out* Posters (1996).

Education Department of Western Australia (1999), Focusing on outcomes: Curriculum Assessment and Reporting, p.85

Eyers, V. (1993), Educating young adolescents. In J. Cumming and D. Flemming (Eds), *In the Middle or at the Centre? A Report on a National Conference on Middle Schooling*, Australian Curriculum Studies Association, Belconnen, ACT.

Eyers, V. *et al.* (1992), *The Education of Young Adolescents in South Australian Government Schools: Report of the Junior School Review*, Adelaide Education Department, South Australia.

Fedlaufer, H., Midgley, C. and Eccles, J. (1998), Students, teacher and observer perceptions of the classroom environment before and after the transition to junior high school, *Journal of Early Adolescence*, pp.133–156.

Fullan, M. and Hargreaves, A. (1991), *Working Together for Your School*, Australian Council for Education Administration, Inc., Paperbacks, Victoria, Australia, pp.52–53.

Galton, M., Gray, J. and Rudduck, J. (1999), *The Impact of School Transitions and Transfers on Pupil Progress and Attainment*, DfEE, London.

Gee, J. (1990), *Social Linguistics and Literacies: Ideology in Discourses*, Falmer Press, London.

Gill, M. (1998), Who set the benchmarks? Analysing the National Literacy Agenda, *English in Australia*, 121.

Ginsburg, H. (1989), *Children's Arithmetic: How They Learn It and How You Teach It*, Pro. Ed., Austin.

Glasser, W. (1993), *The Quality School Teacher*, HarperCollins, New York.

Goodman, Y. (1985), Kid Watching: Observing in the Classroom. In A. Jagger and M. Smith-Bourke, *Observing the Language Learner*, Newark, DE: International Reading Association.

Green, B. and Bigum, C. (1993), Aliens in the classroom, *Australian Journal of Education*, 37 (2), pp.119–141.

Halliday, M.A.K. (1973), *Learning How to Mean: Exploration in the Development of Language,* Arnold, London.

Hardy, J. and Klarwein, D. (1990), *Written Genres in the Secondary School*, Department of Education, Queensland.

Hargreaves, A. (1998), Middle Schooling 'Communicate clear messages', *The West Australian*, Monday, October 19, 1998. (Reporter: K Ashworth).

Heinemann (1996), *Outcomes: Science Books 1–4.*

Heinemann (1998), *Outcomes: Studies of Society and Environment.*

Hill, P. (1993), *School and Teacher Effectiveness in Victoria: Key Findings of the Victorian Quality Schools Project*, University of Melbourne, Melbourne.

Hill, P. and Crevola, C. (1999), Characteristics of an effective literacy strategy, *Unicorn*, 24 (2), August.

Kenworthy, C. and Kenworthy, S. (1997), *Changing Places – Aboriginality in Texts and Contexts*, Fremantle Arts Press, Western Australia.

Kiddey, P. (1995), School Literacy Report.

Kiddey, P. (1998), 'Factors which impact on middle school students as they tackle the literacy demands of different learning areas', Masters Project, Edith Cowan University, Western Australia.

Kiddey, P. (2000), So what's different about learning in the middle and secondary school context?, *Journal of the Australian Literacy Educators' Association*, 8 (1), Melbourne, Victoria.

Kirkpatrick, D. (1995), 'The transition from primary to secondary school: Self regulated learning and achievement motivation', Ph.D. thesis, Edith Cowan University, Western Australia.

Kress, G. (1985), *Linguistic Processes in Sociocultural Practice*, Deakin University, Victoria.

Kress, G. (1996), New London Group, A pedagogy of multiliteracies: Designing social futures, *Harvard Educational Review*, 66 (1), pp.60–91.

Kress, G. (1999). Cited in C. Wyatt-Smith and J. Cumming, Examining the literacy demands of the enacted curriculum, *Literacy Learning: Secondary Thoughts*, 7 (2).

Lemke, J. (1995), *Textual Politics: Discourse and Social Dynamics,* Taylor and Francis, London.

Lemke, J. (1999). Cited in C. Wyatt-Smith and J. Cumming, Examining the literacy demands of the enacted curriculum, *Literacy Learning: Secondary Thoughts*, 7 (2).

Lountain, K. and Dumbleton, M. (1999a), On home territory, *Education Quarterly*, Issue 4, Summer, Curriculum Corporation, Victoria.

Lountain, K. and Dumbleton, M. (1999b), Unlocking literacy, *Education Quarterly*, Issue 4, Summer, Curriculum Corporation, Victoria.

Luke, A. (1995), Multimedia: Multiliteracies, *Education Australia*, Issue 30, James Cook University, Queensland.

Martin, J.R. (1985), *Factual Writing: Exploring and Challenging Social Reality,* Deakin University, (Waurn Ponds) Victoria.

Masters, G. and Forster, M. (1996), *Developmental Assessment Resource Kit*, Australian Council of Educational Research, Victoria, Australia.

MCTP Professional Development Package: Assessment Alternatives in Mathematics, EDWA, Perth.

Milan, A. (1998), White Christmas turkey, *The West Australian*, Perth.

Morgan, P. (1993), The time has come, *National Schools (Australia) Network Issues*, Paper No. 1.

Morris, A. and Stewart-Dore, N. (1984), *Learning to Learn from Text: Effective Reading in the Content Areas*, Addison-Wesley, NSW.

Murphy, C. (1997), Finding time for faculties to study together, *Journal of Staff Development*, Summer.

New London Group (1996), A pedagogy of multiliteracies: Designing social futures, *Harvard Educational Review*, 66 (1), pp.60–91.

NSW Department of School Education (1997), *Literacy 97 Strategy, Focus on Literacy*.

Oodles of Noodles (1996), Curriculum Corporation, Carlton, Victoria.

Pressley, M. (2000), Comprehensive instruction in elementary school: A quarter century of research progress. In *Reading for Meaning; Fostering Comprehension in the Middle Grades,* Teachers College Press, IRA Newark, DE19714.

Project of National Significance (1996), *National MSA Newsletter*, Australian Curriculum Studies Association.

Pupils, SA Field Study, 1994, Project of National Significance (1996), *National Middle School Association Newsletter.*

Reid, J., Forrestal, P. and Cook, J. (1989), *Small Group Learning in the Classroom*, Primary English Association – Chalkface Press, Western Australia.

Rosenholtz, S. (1989), *Teachers' Workplace: The Social Organisation of Schools*, Longman, New York.

Rosenthal, R. and Jacobsen, L. (1968), *Teacher Attitudes towards Students are Vitally Important in Shaping the Self Concepts of Students,* Longman, New York.

Rosenthal, R. and Jacobsen, L. (1968), *Pygmalion in the Classroom: Teacher Expectation and Pupils' Intellectual Development*, Holt, Rhinehart and Winston, New York.

Rudduck, J., Chaplain, R. and Wallace, C. (1996), *School Improvement: What Can Pupils Tell Us?*, Fulton, London.

SA Field Study (1994), as reported in *Curriculum Perspectives*, 15 (2), June, 1995, Australian Curriculum Studies Association.

Sawyer, W. (1999), Testing the benchmarks, Literacy and Year 7, *English in Australia*, 124.

Schools Council Report (1990), State Board of Education, Victoria, p.24. In *Schools Council Document* p.87.

Schulz C. (1960), Peanuts Cartoon United Feature Syndicate, Inc.

Simpson, B., *The Simpons* (C and TM), Twentieth Century Fox Film Corporation. All Rights Reserved.

Snyder, I. (1996), Integrating computers into the literacy curriculum: More difficult than we first imagined, *Australian Journal of Language and Literacy*, 19 (4), pp.330–344.

South Australian Film Corporation, *Lingo Video*, Film and Video Distribution, 3 Butler Drive, Westside Commercial Centre, Tapleys Hill Road, Heydon, South Australia, 5014.

Spender, D. (1995), *Nattering on the Net: Women, Power and Cyberspace*, Spinifex Press, North Melbourne.

Stenmark, J. (1991), *Mathematics Assessment: Myths, Models, Good Questions, and Practical Suggestions*, National Council of Teachers of Mathematics, Virginia, USA.

Vygotsky, L.S. (1978), *Mind in Society: The Development of Higher Mental Psychological Processes*, Harvard University Press, Cambridge, MA.

Vygotsky, L.S. (1978), *Mind in Society*, MIT Press, Cambridge, MA.

Vygotsky, L.S. (1966), *Thought and Language* (A. Kozulin, Trans), MIT Press, Cambridge, MA.

Vygotsky, L.S. (1986), *Thought and Language* (New Edition), Harvard University Press, Cambridge, MA.

Warhurst, J. (1994), Understanding cross curricular practice in schools, *ACSA Occasional Paper*, December, Paper No. 5.

Westwood, P. (1995), Teachers' beliefs and expectations concerning students with learning difficulties, *Australian Journal of Remedial Education*, 27 (2), pp.19–21.

Wilson, B. (1999), Schooling: What matters?, *Education Quarterly*, Summer, Curriculum Corporation, Melbourne, Editorial, p.3.

Wilson, J. and Wing Jan, L. (1993), *Thinking for Themselves, Developing Strategies for Reflective Learning*, Eleanor Curtain Publishing, Armadale, Victoria.

Winton, T. (1990), *Lockie Leonard, Human Torpedo*, Puffin Books, Melbourne.

Winton, T. (1993), *Lockie Leonard, Scumbuster*, Piper Pan McMillan, Australia.

Wyatt-Smith, C. and Cumming, J. (1999), Examining the literacy demands of the enacted curriculum, *Literacy Learning: Secondary Thoughts*, 7 (2).

Index

Stepping Out Training Courses

TUTOR TRAINING COURSE

The *Stepping Out* Tutor Training Course is a five day course in which participants develop in-depth understandings of literacy issues and learning strategies. In addition, the course addresses the role of the 'literacy leader' within a school, how to co-ordinate whole school or department literacy planning and how to run workshops for school staff.

INTRODUCTORY SESSION

Learning in the Middle and Secondary School

Includes

- the challenges facing adolescent learners and why they have difficulties
- factors which facilitate learning
- the impact of school structures
- the benefits of a whole-school or department focus for improving performance.

WRITING SESSIONS

Include

- Monitoring pupils' writing
- Subject-specific spelling
- Written genres in the middle and secondary school context
- A problem solving approach to writing
- Journal writing in learning areas
- Implementing writing strategies in everyday teaching

READING SESSIONS

Include

- What matters in reading and viewing
- An introduction to critical literacy
- Selecting texts for the middle and secondary school
- Using note-making frameworks
- Portfolio assessment
- Implementing reading and viewing strategies in everyday teaching.

IMPLEMENTATION SESSIONS

Include

- The role of the tutor as a change agent
- Subject area and whole-school planning and improvement

FOR INFORMATION OR BOOKINGS   TEL 01865 314055

TWO-DAY TEACHER COURSE

The *Stepping Out* Two-Day Course, in either Reading for Writing, trains subject teachers in implementing *Stepping Out* strategies to improve pupils' performance in their own learning area.

Two-Day Courses are available on request for a group or 20 teachers or more, at a local venue. Courses run from 9.00 am to 4.30 pm daily.

WRITING COURSE

Includes

- Monitoring pupils' writing
- Subject-specific spelling
- Written genres in the middle and secondary school context
- A problem solving approach to writing
- Journal writing in learning areas
- Implementing writing strategies in everyday teaching

READING COURSE

Includes

- What matters in reading and viewing
- An introduction to critical literacy
- Selecting texts for the middle and secondary school
- Using note-making frameworks
- Portfolio assessment
- Implementing reading and viewing strategies in everyday teaching.

STEPPING OUT INFORMATION SEMINARS

Information seminars provide a succinct introduction to *Stepping Out* to help inform your decision about training. Lasting approximately one and a half hours you can attend a pre-arranged seminar, or request we hold one of a group of teachers in your area.

FAX 01865 314116   WEB www.ghpd.co.uk

Other *Stepping Out* Resources

READING: STRATEGIES FOR SUCCESS

This book examines the key reading and learning strategies and how all secondary teachers can use them in their subject teaching.

It focuses on

- the reading/writing connection and how this informs teaching

- what matters in reading and viewing, including a summary of the key skills, e.g. skimming and scanning, note-making and text reconstruction.

- applying a reading and viewing framework. How to enhance understanding of written texts, e.g. previewing, silent reading, guided reading and summarising.

- selecting texts and the criteria for matching texts to a range of pupils' ability

- using note-making frameworks such as diagramming, graphic outlines and structured overviews.

- an introduction to critical literacy and ways to improve comprehension of subject material at all levels

- monitoring pupils' reading through observation, checklists and analysis, to inform planning and teaching

ISBN 0435 047094

WRITING: STRATEGIES FOR SUCCESS

This is practical resource book for all subject teachers. It examines a range of writing and learning strategies and how to use them in everyday teaching to make learning more effective. Practical examples are given throughout.

It focuses on

- the writing process, including a summary of the key skills, e.g. note-making, drafting and revising.

- a problem-solving approach to wrtiing and how to help pupils understand and apply the features used by writers at text, sentence and word level.

- written genre, covering thirteen common genre of the secondary curriculum, e.g. historical recount, mathematics and science investigation, discussion and argument.

- journal writing and how it enhances content understanding.

ISBN 0435 047108

- spelling and how to include subject specific spelling strategies in everyday teaching.

- monitoring pupils' writing through portfolios of work to inform planning and teaching.